Maheeba

To.
My dear friend E n.
Happy WLAC.
love Evelyn

Maheeba

✦

From the Middle East to Middle America

Evelyn M. Price

iUniverse, Inc.
New York Lincoln Shanghai

Maheeba
From the Middle East to Middle America

iUniverse, Inc.

For information address:
iUniverse, Inc.
2021 Pine Lake Road, Suite 100
Lincoln, NE 68512
www.iuniverse.com

ISBN: 0-595-31525-9

Printed in the United States of America

Contents

Introduction

How did I, the daughter of two people who came from the Middle East as adults, become just an average American woman? I can still hear my mother, Maheeba, admonishing me to be a "good Syrian girl" as she worried about possible unbecoming activity in public or in college. Maheeba was caught between two worlds, the conservative society of Arab Christians in a small village in Syria and the evolving communities of urban Ohio. <u>Maheeba: from the Middle East to Middle America</u> is based on the story of a woman who journeyed across the ocean and across time, leaving a way of life that had not changed in hundreds of years for a culture not yet clearly defined. The episodes are true, as I remember them, but the timing and setting may not be accurate.

Syria was governed by the Ottoman Empire at the time of my parent's immigration. Under Turkish rule, Syria was a target for ethnic cleansing, massacres, and cruelty. In the midst of a tense society, Maheeba remembers a happy childhood although she became the caretaker of her father and four brothers at the age of ten, after the death of her mother. Maheeba did not see her difficult life as a burden, but found fulfillment in serving the men in her life, as was expected of Syrian women. It is this male dominated culture that she brought with her to America, and which profoundly influenced my life.

I was the youngest child, five years younger than my sister; my mother had time to spend with me. She filled my world with stories of her life; sharing her thoughts, and feelings about growing up, to the age of thirteen, in Syria. My mother's culture and religion were one, and she modeled her role well.

Had I not gone to college, Maheeba might have molded me into a "good Syrian girl" like my sisters. Instead, I was often at odds with my mother. Her idea of a "good Syrian girl" was in conflict with my version of the "all American girl". I rebelled against my mother's disturbing superstitions and her beliefs in curses and the evil eye. But beyond these conflicts, I found her life to be romantic and adventurous. She was a beautiful bride who watched her brilliant, loving husband descend suddenly into mental illness, leaving her alone to care for her family. This book describes how she and her family survive, the pain of broken dreams and the power of superstition, through the strength of love.

Names have been changed to protect my family's privacy.

Arabic language

The use of Arabic words in the text may need explanation. *Allah* is the Arabic word for God. While it is commonly thought to mean the Islamic God, all Arabic speakers, Christian and Muslim, refer to their God as *Allah*. *Min shan Allah*, "For the sake of God," was an often-used phrase to persuade my brothers to eat more food. My mother would repeat, "For my sake, for your father," and then finally, *min shan Allah*.

Translating Arabic to English can be confusing, for example, *mezza, mezzeh*, and *maza* all mean appetizers, and can be used interchangeably. *Tata* is grandmother, and Mheeba always referred to her own mother as *Ime*, Arabic for "mother."

There is no "o" sound in Arabic, but sometimes Muslim is spelled Moslem, Muhammad as Mohammed and Quran as Koran. When writing Arabic words I tried to spell them phonetically, so the reader could pronounce them.

1

Portsmouth, Ohio, 1934

I was four years old, living in Portsmouth, Ohio. By 1934, Europe was witnessing the rising tide of Nazism and Chamberlain was promising "peace in our time." The United States was beginning to crawl out of the deep hole of the Depression with Roosevelt's New Deal.

My family was feeling the full blow of the economic collapse. Like many emigrants, the Thomas's story of rags-to-riches-to-rags was echoed throughout the land—the American dream realized and lost in fifteen short years.

I never experienced the "good life." My father's, house of cards fell before I was born. He had invested heavily in real estate and in the stock market. After purchasing a building, he would mortgage it to finance another, always paying cash for the new property.

We were poor. I was the youngest of nine children living in a dilapidated, dingy, bug-infested, old hotel on Main Street. It was the only piece of property to survive my father's vast holdings, and it was mortgaged for $7,000.

In contrast to the decaying walls, we enjoyed beautiful, state-of-the-art furniture, which had not been repossessed. I remember the plush green velvet sofa, love seat, hand carved coffee tables and Queen Ann chairs. Mom's beautiful treasure chest was built from the cedars of Lebanon. I think she would open it just to inhale the aromas of her homeland. All that was left were memories.

We had an enormous round oak table with huge carved "elephant" legs. Mom said she wanted a table big enough to dance on, and I think the whole family could have danced on this one. With the twelve matching chairs, the table dominated the dining room. It left little space for the cherry wood china closet and ice box.

A ray of soft sunlight beamed through the pane of the large glass window, streamed around the room and focused on the cracked black and yellow linoleum. It provided the only source of natural light in the adjacent kitchen.

There was a yellow and white enamel gas stove with an attached compartment for burning coal. Maheeba, my mother, stoked the fire every morning, adding coal as needed to take the chill off the morning air. Our only cupboard had exposed shelves and held all the spices and food stuff. I mastered the art of shelf climbing to retrieve the hidden sugar bowl.

Facing the stove was a white porcelain sink with a drain board on each side. It had a rusty faucet for cold water. We had no hot water heater. A blue and white print skirt wrapped around the front of the sink, hiding the crock of fermenting raisins called *arak*.

I was unaware of the world situation and oblivious to my surroundings. I was home alone with my mother, content, after my siblings had gone to work or school. I remember sitting at the dining table in my bare feet and faded night-gown. My pigtails were still intact from the day before. The table was set with olives and cheese. Mom tore off a piece of Syrian bread and spread it with butter and home made jelly. I tilted my head back, held the treasured bread over my open mouth and squeezed. My tongue caught the golden drops of melted butter.

My mother serenaded me with "Syria the Beautiful in Arabic." As she moved around the room, she would pinch my cheeks and stroke my hair. I joined in the chorus. All too soon, her performance was interrupted by a knock on the door.

Mom put a cup of hot cocoa in front of me. "Add some cold milk, it's too hot," she yelled over her shoulder.

I did as I was told and then dipped my bread into warm cocoa. My brothers called this Syrian Wheaties. They drank coffee with lots of milk.

"Come in, Edna," I could hear my mother say. "We'll get started right away. I have the wallpaper in the living room."

"Fine, I have the brushes and paste, everything I need," said the stranger whose voice was low and masculine.

"Oh this is your little girl," Edna said, bending down to grab my hand. "Hi honey."

Her husky voice sounded like Daddy. She was dressed in a straight, faded pink flowered dress, which suited her skinny figure. She had a flat chest, thin lips and hairy arms which covered thick bones. She wore heavy tan cotton stockings with black-laced shoes. Her coarse gray hair, receding at the hairline, was pulled back into a bun. Not like any woman I knew! Most unusual were her pale gray-blue eyes, set in a face whose expression appeared cruel to me.

"Don't get in the way," Mom said. "Edna will be very busy."

"Oh, she won't bother me. I love children," Edna said.

Edna hauled her materials and equipment into the living room, and looked over the existing wallpaper. "I'll just paper over this," she said. "I'll scrape off any loose paper and sand it smooth. Maheeba, is this the only room you want me to do?"

"Yes, for now," Mom answered.

Edna placed two chairs facing each other and laid a plank the width of the roll of paper between them. She set out a wide brush and then poured some dry paste into a bucket. She took the bucket into the kitchen, added water, and stirred the mixture until it was smooth. Shifting slightly in my chair, I turned my head and gazed at her. Edna smiled at me as I studied the lines of her face. Her eyes were opaque, no depth, unlike the dark brown eyes I knew and trusted.

"I have to run to the neighbor next door for a few minutes. I won't be long," Mom said to Edna. Stopping in the kitchen, she wiped my face. "Be good. Don't bother the busy lady. I'll be right back."

I climbed down from the table, walked into the living room and stood watching Edna work. She brushed paste on a panel of wallpaper and folded it over her arm. Climbing the ladder, she pressed the top part firmly to the wall, and let the rest of it fall naturally. She then brushed the paper smooth with a coarse brush to seal it.

"Come over here and I'll let you stir the paste," the lady said. "Don't be afraid. I like little girls. Come here and give Aunt Edna a hug."

"I hope I don't have to hug her," I thought. I always kissed my Aunts, and just about every adult woman who came to the house, on the cheek. I didn't really mind because they often gave me candy or things. But Edna was strange and I didn't like her.

I watched as Edna put her equipment down. She walked over, picked me up and kissed me on the lips. I didn't resist but no one ever kissed me on the lips, not even Mama.

"She smells like Daddy's old smoke," I thought. "Her face hurts, it scratches me. She's not soft like Mama and no big bosoms. I don't like her."

She sat me down, and knelt in front of me. "Give me a kiss," she said. I stepped back. "Don't be afraid honey. Give Aunt Edna a kiss."

She grabbed me, hugged me tight, and kissed me hard. She tried to stick her tongue into my mouth. I couldn't escape her grasp. As she tightened her grip with her left arm, she ran her other hand up my dress, following the thigh and into my panties. She fingered my vagina. I struggled.

I couldn't speak. "You're not allowed to do that." My mind was racing. "Mama will be mad at you," I thought. Then she rubbed the nipples on my flat little breasts and back down again. I was terrified. I struggled to get loose but couldn't move. Edna kissed me harder.

"Stop it! No," I cried inside. "I don't like you. You're a bad lady. Mama make her stop." My heart was beating fast and hard. I could hardly breathe.

"You feel so good. Relax. This is fun," Edna said, forcing me to lie down.

I managed to wiggle free. Trying to stop me, Edna fell flat on the floor. I ran to my mother's bedroom and into the closet. I crouched down far in the back and buried my face in Mama's dress. I could smell bread flour and lilac. "Don't find me. I'll tell on you. Go away you bad lady," I cried softly. "Mama, Mama, help me." I held Mama's dress to my mouth to stifle the tears. There was an eerie silence and then a voice.

"Honey, come see Aunt Edna, don't be afraid," she called, struggling to get up off her knees. "I won't hurt you. I'll give you candy."

I could hear her foot steps coming into the bedroom and then stop. "Are you under the bed? Come on honey. I have candy."

I tried to stem my sobs, catching my breath in little spasms. "Stay away you bad lady. I'll tell on you. My brother will beat you up. He can knock you down and hurt you. I hate you, I hate you."

Just then I heard the back door open. Mama's home! Her picture flashed in my mind. Edna hurried back to work.

"How are you doing?" I heard Mama ask. "Where is Ellen?"

"Mama," I cheered, as I ran to my mother and grabbed her leg.

She picked me up. "Are you ok?"

I stared at Edna. Her pupils enlarged. The glassy, almost colorless eyes didn't seem real. They looked like big marbles. She had an icy glare. "It's the evil eye, like Mama talked about," I thought. "You're a bad lady. I want to tell Mama on you. I want Phil to beat you up. But I'm afraid of you. You'll kill us."

I knew that the evil eye caused headaches, and diarrhea. Once when we were in a grocery store, a clerk starred at us. He may have been wondering if I was going to shop lift the candy bar in my hand. Mom picked me up, put the candy back, and pressed my head into her chest, shielding me from harm. She hurried out of the store. "What's the matter?" I asked.

"He has the evil eye," she said.

Now, I recalled, his eyes were light blue.

I could feel Edna's eyes penetrating my body. I put my arms around my mother's neck and hugged her tight. Mama carried me into the kitchen and we sat at the table. "I'll fix you some chocolate milk."

There was always a pan of homemade chocolate syrup on the stove. We never drank plain milk. I sipped the delightful drink, and looked at my mother. "Where is your mommy?" I asked.

"She died in Syria, a long time ago."

"Did she know me?"

"No," Mom said. "I was a young girl, about ten years old when she died. Why?"

"Was it the evil eye?"

Mama acquired a blank look of concentration as she drifted into the past. "I don't know. Sometimes I thought maybe. My Ime, your grandmother, was sick a lot. Not like a cough or stomach ache. She got tired. We would be dancing and she would stop to rest. Sometimes she stayed in bed for days. Something or someone made her tired. I wondered if it was our neighbor, Seloma. She was jealous of my mother. The evil eye is a curse. Some people don't know they have it until they cause sickness."

"Maheeba, I'm ready to go now," Edna said, standing in the doorway. "I'm all finished, unless you have something else,"

"I'll get your money. I'll let you know if we need you."

I covered my eyes and laid my head down on the table, wondering if the evil eye had killed my grandmother. Trying not to think of Edna, I filled my head with visions of the beautiful Syria that Mom had described. There were fruit trees, olive groves, grape arbors, and fields of golden wheat; unlike our victory garden of potted vegetables on the porch. They had sheep and goats. I wondered, "What was my grandmother like? She died when mama was little, a long time ago. I wish I was there now."

2

Hums, Syria, 1904

Syria is situated on the shores of the Mediterranean—birthplace of Jesus, land of the Apostles and Prophets. At the turn of the twentieth century, it was mostly a sandy desert with patches of grassy plains.

Once a Christian country, it had been invaded by the Muslim Turks. The reality of Ethnic cleansing, the massacres of Christians and Jews were stories rewritten in today's headlines. Syria then, as today, was a land of conflict within itself and with the Western World.

Along the fertile Ghuta River valley, in a 400 square mile oasis was the small village of Hums, where my mother, was born. It was an island surrounded by a sea of sand. The soil there was rich and the villagers, who worked it, built their beehive-shaped houses of stone or sun-dried bricks. The flat roofs over the entrance were used to dry fruits and vegetables.

On this day in the fall, like any other day before dawn, the villagers were asleep. The sky was clear. It promised to be a hot day. A few animals were stirring. The roosters had not yet crowed to announce the beginning of a new day.

Only in one house, bigger than most and smaller than a few, one of the occupants was moving around. He had not slept.

A flicker of candlelight moved, stopped, moved, stopped. The light roved from room to room. The absence of windows amplified the darkness. The single candle lit up an entire room. He glanced into the bedroom where his three sons slept on floor mats. The clay floors silenced his foot steps. Then he stopped.

"Maheeba! Maheeba!" The man's voice had broken the silence. "Wake up." He shook his sleeping daughter.

"Go away. Let me sleep. I feel so nice and warm." The child rolled her face into her pillow to shut out the sharp sound of his voice in its hollow cave. "Go away," she dreamed of shouting back. "I don't want to get up."

"Maheeba!"

The child sat straight up, startled by her father's harsh voice. The room was dark; except for the candle he held which illuminated his face. He looked tired, very tired. His well-trimmed beard was wet and she could see the tears in his eyes.

"Papa, what's the matter?"

"Dress quickly, go to your brother Hashar and tell him to come here. Now."

"Is it *Ime*?"

"Yes. It's your mother." Without another word, he carefully lit the candle beside his daughter's bed from his own. *Yella, yella,* hurry, hurry, he mumbled. His huge shadow followed him out the door.

Obediently, Maheeba pulled off her nightgown and groped in the dimly lighted room for her blue dress, faded from the sun and frequent laundering. Like all of her dresses, the design was straight and loose-fitting. To expose a girl's figure was a breach of modesty. Not that her own flat chest could be considered alluring. Putting it on, she rubbed her hands down the front to smooth out the wrinkles. Then she sat on the edge of the bed to slip on her long pants and old, dusty brown sandals.

Standing up she licked her hands and brushed a few loose hairs back off of her face. The rest of her black hair was neatly contained in one long braid. She reached for her *hatla*, tied it under her chin and blew out the candle. On the right hand side of the front door hung an eight-inch wooden cross of Jesus. She kissed her fingertips then touched the feet of Christ. "Allah be with me," she whispered. Quietly closing the door behind her, she set out on her journey.

Maheeba tried not to think about her mother but it was impossible to suppress the fear. She remembered the day they were picking tomatoes. Ime had dropped her basket and had fallen to the ground. She had grabbed her chest and struggled to breathe. Ime had been sick for a long time before that day. She would get tired and stay in bed for days. "I wonder if it's the evil eye," Maheeba thought. "Papa said her heart was old and wearing out. Maybe Confidad can make her well."

The sun, which had not yet broken through the clouds, made its presence known by illuminating one big, bright silver cloud.

Hashar lived just a few blocks away. The houses were close together, saving all the land for farming and herding. The closeness to neighbors created an extended family, working and playing together. It was almost time to "swap" children for work. Maheeba knew that every year, Papa would take her brothers to the sheep herder and say, "Look my boys are strong and will work hard. Two boys, tough like four men. They take your sheep to market." The sheepherder, in exchange, would send his daughters to help Papa pick his ripe fruits and vegetables. The girls would sort through the produce, picking the best for market and setting aside others to be dried.

Maheeba began to run as fast as she could, not looking at the neighboring houses, although she knew everyone in the village. Her family had lived here for generations. The night air was cool. Rubbing her arms, she said, "I wish I had brought my long, warm, *abeyah*. But when the sun comes out, it will be another hot day."

Maheeba sensed the village was strangely quiet. She knew it would be a few more hours before the houses emptied into the court yard, everyone visiting and working.

She passed the well, the focal point of the village, where every one got their water. "I'm thirsty," she whispered, "but can't stop." Passing the wheat fields, she said, "I remember when I was little, shorter than the wheat. I would creep up behind Ime, and make squeaking sounds.

"There's a mouse, help," Ime would scream.

"I can see myself jumping up and down laughing."

This time of the year the gardens were full with big ripe melons and vegetables. Papa would say, many times, "Give a Syrian water and he will grow the most luscious fruits on Earth". Most of the houses had apricots and dates laid out to dry on the flat roofs. "I'll bet our nuts are dried by now," Maheeba said. "Papa will want us to take them in and put the fruits out." Her trend of thought was broken by the crowing of a rooster, one then another, like an echo.

"Maheeba!" a neighbor called, "Slow down, I give you some apricots."

"Can't, got to get Hashar!"

The neighbor stood up and made the sign of the cross, "It must be bad news. Allah be with you."

Arriving at her destination, Maheeba banged on the door. She could hear the family moving around. Finally the door opened. It was Confidad, her sister-in-law, carrying her nine-month-old baby and looking surprised to see Maheeba. "Oh, in the name of Allah, what's wrong? It's your mother, I can feel it. Hashar! Yella, yella, we have to go to your father's house. Take Mykhal. I get ready."

Maheeba reached out to her little nephew. Smiling she patted his beautiful red curly hair and kissed him on the cheek. She followed Confidad to the kitchen and watched her gather a few things and put the bread dough in a bowl.

"I'll make bread there. Do you need bread?"

"I think so. I made bread a couple of days ago."

"Oh, the way you make bread, like little dishes. Don't they teach you how to make real thin Syrian bread in school? It's a shame; you don't have *Tata,* grandmother, to teach you."

"I'm only ten," Maheeba said. "I tried to twirl the bread dough in the air and it fell on the floor. Some day I'll be able to make bread just like my Ime."

Confidad hadn't even listened; she was off to the bedroom.

Hashar appeared buttoning up his full length shirt. "Is it Ime?"

"I think so," Maheeba answered.

"Did you eat breakfast?"

"No."

"Eat, eat, there's bread, olives, cheese, fruit."

Maheeba put Mykhal on the floor and tore off a piece of bread, smeared it with butter and rolled it up to eat. Until now she hadn't realized how hungry she was.

Confidad returned, dressed all in black; dress, robe, and scarf. She was tall and slender, unlike most village women. She picked up Mykhal, wiped his face, then grabbed one bag and nodded to Maheeba to grab the other. As they passed through the door, each one touched the hanging wooden cross for protection.

Maheeba grabbed her sister-in-law's hand. "Confidad means healer. Will you make Ime well?"

"I cure headaches and drive off evil eye. Your mother is sick a long time. It's in Allah's hands. Hashar, look! They are drying apricots and dates. We need to get ours ready."

"You have to get the wheat and onions off the roof," Hashar said. "Aren't they dry yet? Then I will put out our fruits and vegetables."

"I wash wheat, it has to dry," Confidad said. "I can't make it go faster."

"Ime is sick, and you fight about drying fruits. I can't stand it," Maheeba said. "I'm going ahead."

By the time she arrived at home, other family members and friends were parading into the house. Maheeba made her way to her mother's room. It was dark and quiet; the women were kneeling, praying and chanting. They bobbed their heads up and down, kissing the crucifix or rosaries in their hands. Her brother, Tomas, was swinging the gold incense burner back and forth, saturating the air with the scented smoke. Maheeba was bewildered and frightened. "What is happening? If only I could see Ime."

FatherYusuf, putting his hands on her shoulder, gently shuffled her out of the room.

"What's wrong with Ime?"

"Nothing you can do," Father said. "Why don't you take your little brother for a walk?"

Maheeba went to the kitchen where Mykhal was sitting with Farouk eating bread and jelly.

"Take the boys out to play," Confidad said. "It will be good for you. I give you a pomegranate and some dried apricots."

"I want one too," insisted Farouk.

Confidad cut a circular cap off of the top of the pomegranate then put the cap back on like a cork. She bent down and handed Farouk the big red ball like fruit. "Now listen to your sister and don't drink the juice until she tells you, hear? It should last till you get home." Confidad put on Farouk's *hatla and akal*, head scarf and coil, to protect him from the sun. Farouk took the precious fruit and nodded. Even at five, he knew what it was like to be thirsty in the desert.

"Hold on to my dress," Maheeba said, picking up Mykhal. "Let's go." As they left the house, Farouk stood on his toes to touch the cross. "Allah be with me."

The trio wondered through the fields of wheat, running and laughing. Farouk ran ahead and hid, then jumped out to scare his sister. They twirled around and dropped to the ground.

"Can we get some dates?" Farouk asked.

"I can't reach the dates," Maheeba said. "They're too high, but I can pick figs." She laid the baby down, and standing on her tiptoes, she picked a big black fig. It burst open exposing the reddish insides with colonies of little black seeds. The fig was large enough to fill Farouk's whole hand. Maheeba broke off a piece of her own and put it in Mykhal's mouth. Like a baby bird, he sucked it up and opened his mouth for more.

Farouk trotted ahead, stopping at an apricot tree. Around and around, he skittered, like a cat chasing its tail. As the other two caught up, Farouk reached for a branch. "Up, up, lift me up."

Maheeba sat the baby down in the tall grass, and then walked over to her brother. She held him up to grab the branch. Farouk giggled as he swung back and forth, back and forth, and then dropped into Maheeba's arms. "Again, again," he begged.

Maheeba looked over and saw Mykhal pick up the pomegranate and suck it. He lay back on the grass and played with his big, red 'ball'.

"It is so peaceful and quiet," she thought. "I wish life could go on forever this way. I have nothing to worry about. Just play in the sun. Maybe Ime will be well when we get home and everything will be like it was. It would be so nice if we could sing and dance again. We were so happy." Suddenly, Maheeba dropped Farouk on the ground and crouched down. She strained her ears to listen.

"Do you hear it?"

"What?"

The sound of thunder was distinctly clear, "Horses, horses! Do you hear them?"

"Yea, yea, horses!" screamed Farouk, jumping up and down.

"No! They might be Turks!"

Frightened, Farouk asked, "Do they really eat children? Bashada said they do."

"I don't know," Maheeba said. "Papa told him not to say such things. But once when I was little like you, I saw a man in the town square. He was tied to a pole, beaten and teased by soldiers. They cut off a piece of skin from his leg and tried to feed it to him. There was so much blood. I couldn't scream, I couldn't cry. It was horrible, too horrible to be real. Papa covered my eyes and took me away."

"Who was the man?" Farouk asked.

"Papa said he was a Christian, accused of attempted assassination. He tried to kill the Sultan." The memory terrified her. "We have to go. Yella, Yella! Go fast, run." She picked up her little nephew and grabbed Farouk's hand. "Run, run." They headed for home. Her adrenalin tripled as she took flight but Farouk couldn't keep up.

The stampede grew louder and louder, closer and closer. Looking behind her, Maheeba saw bright red tassels swinging from gray hats. There were two Turkish soldiers. This was Maheeba's worse nightmare. She'd heard her father and brothers talk about the massacres. Whole villages had been wiped out, men and women slaughtered. Children sacrificed or kidnapped. The soldiers were known as the Terrible Turks.

"In the name of Allah, don't let them catch us, please Allah, please," Maheeba prayed. "I wish we could be home now with Papa. Maybe we should have stayed hidden in the tall grass. We were safer there. Can't out run them. Now what do we do? The Terrible Turks, they're coming, coming to get us. Come on Farouk we are going to hide in those bushes. Yella, yella, we can't beat them. Hide."

The three children huddled together under a bush. Maheeba tried to shield them with her body and prayed, "Don't see us, go away, please Allah make them go away."

Silence. The horses had stopped. With her head bent, Maheeba looked under her arm and saw the long, brown, slender legs of a horse. She could hear the horses snorting, and Mykhal began to cry. She held him close, but could not move. Her heart was beating so fast, she felt chest pains. She was too petrified to cry.

"Don't be afraid children. We won't hurt you." The soldiers dismounted and the first one lifted Maheeba off of her brother. The soldiers, dressed in beautiful red and gray uniforms, were smiling. They looked harmless, even friendly.

Without warning, Farouk jumped up and kicked the first soldier. The soldier grabbed Farouk, lifted him up and held him in the air.

"What shall we do with this little lion? Maybe we should cut off his balls." Farouk clutched his privates. "Look, look, He knows what you said," the second soldier laughed.

Maheeba picked up the baby. Her heart was beating hard and fast, "Please, please," she begged with tears in her eyes. "He's my brother."

The soldier put Farouk down. "We won't hurt you. We really don't eat children," he said patting the boy on the head. "They're too tough." Then he reached over to Mykhal, smiled, spit on his hands, rubbed them together and stroked the child's red hair. "It is good luck," he said.

"Do you know that you are lucky to have red hair?" the second soldier said as he rubbed Mykhal's head. The baby reached for the soldier's tassel, but he pulled away.

"We must go now. Be careful and watch that spitfire kid brother."

The soldiers mounted their horses and rode away. Maheeba fell to her knees. With three fingers she made the sign of the cross. Then she got up and, took Farouk's hand angrily. "Let's go home."

"They were Turks, real soldiers," Farouk said. "Wait till I tell Papa. I can tell Papa can't I?"

"Be quiet. You almost got us in trouble. Now hurry up."

"I want my juice," Farouk cried. "I'm thirsty."

"Alright!" Maheeba was thirsty too. It was time to have a treat. She squeezed her pomegranate and let the juice run into Mykhal's mouth, then took a sip herself. Farouk enjoyed having his own, and made loud slurping sounds. Then she gave everyone a dried apricot and continued homeward.

When they got home, Farouk pulled away from his sister and ran to the house, yelling, "Papa, Papa!"

The house was filled with a thick haze of sweet smelling incense. It was cold and quiet, except for the muffled sound of women wailing.

"Shhhh", one of the ladies whispered guiding Farouk out of the house. When she saw Maheeba, she hugged her, took the baby and began to wail, "You poor child, you will have to be Ime now."

Maheeba pushed her away and ran to the house. She knew, with the house dark, the smell of incense, the crying and the wailing, she knew. Death was lurking everywhere. She clutched her waist. It felt like a sharp sword had pierced her heart. Her knees weakened and she dropped to the floor. "No, no, it can't be real," she cried. "Ime, Ime, don't leave me."

Maheeba did not even try to go into her mother's room. There would be lots of time to view the lifeless body, with a wake that would last for two days. Already the people were coming with food. Instead, Maheeba went outside, sat on the step and began to cry.

Farouk joined his sister and hugged her.

"Where's Ime?" Farouk asked, pouting. "I want Ime."

He looked frightened, holding back tears. "Ime's not here." Maheeba didn't know what to say to him. He was too young to understand. "I want Ime too."

She sat him on her lap, held him close, "Ime is gone. She won't be here in the morning. When *Umtee,* aunt Dalal died, she never came back."

"Ime, I need you," she whispered. "Who will I talk to—dance with—sing? I have no one. What will happen now?" Maheeba put her head in her hands, and cried. The rest of the day's events were forgotten.

"Come on Farouk," Confidad said. "I'll get you something to eat. Maheeba, come too."

Maheeba didn't even hear her sister-in-law. She got up and began to run out into the fields. "I have to get away from these people," she said. She ran and ran until she dropped. "Ime, where are you? I am so scared," she cried. "Please Allah; let me see her one more time." She waited and waited. It was dark before Maheeba returned home. If her absence had been noticed, it was not mentioned.

In bed that night she prayed and cried, prayed and cried, until there were no more tears. "Ime, I need you," she muttered over and over. Gradually, she felt herself moving through time and space into a twilight zone, between sleep and consciousness.

"Maheeba, Maheeba!"

"Ime? Where are you?"

"Come my daughter."

She could see, faint at first, then very clear, her mother in the kitchen. She was wearing a pale blue robe, with a black cord tied around the waist. The long, full sleeves were slit to the shoulders. On her upper arm was a slave snake bracelet with ruby eyes.

"Ime!"

"Come, we make bread."

She watched her mother toss the dough rhythmically over one arm, then the other to stretch it. With two hands above her head she twirled the dough around, and then handed it to Maheeba. She tossed the dough over her arm, and then tried to twirl it in the air, but lost control and it came down on her head. They laughed as they picked the sticky dough out of her hair.

Ime picked up a pan and began beating a familiar rhythm. "Come my daughter," she smiled. "Dance for me."

Maheeba whirled around, shook her shoulders and hips like a belly dancer. At the end of the performance, Ime clapped.

Putting the drum away, she got out her castanets. "Dubkee," she said as she grabbed her daughter's hand. Together they sidestepped, swayed, kicked and hopped in a line dance, until they were exhausted and collapsed on the floor. Maheeba's face was flushed. She was so happy. Her body felt weightless.

"Ime, sing me the song about the small man who cheated on his big fat wife."

"I see you hiding behind the door," she sang in Arabic, with the gestures of an opera star. "You scoundrel, I will take the hair from your mustache and beard to make a broom that will sweep my house clean."

"That's so funny, I want to learn it. There is so much I want to know. How did you get Papa?"

"The Bakeers had two handsome sons, *Umee,* uncle Abraham and Papa, who was younger and the best. Everyone was after Papa. The big dowries they offered, it was shameful. But Papa wanted me, just me. My father could only give two sheep. My Ime said that wasn't enough, so she added her own jewelry, my bracelet. She wanted everyone to know that I was special. Papa said he would have married me without a dowry. The women in the village were jealous, especially Seloma. To this day she doesn't like me."

"But she is married."

"Look what she got," Ime said, nudging Maheeba with her elbow.

"Who will I marry? Not Yusuf, son of Sabb, he has a wart on his nose and he orders his sister around all the time."

"He wants to act like a ram."

"Please," Maheeba said, "make some coffee and read my fortune."

"I can tell your future without coffee. I dream for you, a good man, handsome, you will give him many sons. Allah will bless you. Many families have asked for your hand, but you are our only daughter and we want to take our time. Papa wants to wait and see if the boys are good providers. You are very lucky to have such a good papa."

"I want to marry someone like Papa," Maheeba said, twirling around.

Ime held her hand. "It is time, I go now."

"Not yet, please stay a little longer, please, please," Maheeba pleaded. But she was already gone. "Ime, come back, come back. Don't leave. Don't leave me." Maheeba sat up in bed and looked around her room. Where is Ime? The kitchen? It was just a dream. "Ime, now I know you can see me. Stay with me always."

3

Ime's wake, 1904

The morning after Maheeba's dream, she got up early and went into Ime's room. She found her father asleep in the chair. "I wonder why they don't leave the body alone," she whispered.

She walked over to her father, and sat at his feet, resting her head on his lap. He opened his eyes and stroked his daughter's hair. She looked up at her father, his face was drawn, and he seemed old and tired, so very tired.

"Papa, can I get you some coffee?"

"No, I will go rest now."

"I will stay with Ime."

He nodded and then left the room.

Ime was on a makeshift altar—a plank of wood braced by two facing chairs at opposite ends. She was covered with white linens flowing to the floor. Maheeba looked at the cold body, with grayish white skin of clay, a statue, like in church, an Angel. "Is this my Ime? You were always happy and strong. You would tell me stories and play games. So much life. How can this be?"

On her mother's chest was a relic, a tiny piece of wood, from the 'true' cross of Jesus, wrapped in white linen and encased in a small glass box.

Maheeba kissed the relic, then picked up the lifeless hand and held it to her cheek. "Ime, I didn't know you were so sick. Was it the evil eye? We were dancing and singing not very long ago. Who will help me make my wedding dress? What if Papa marries again and she doesn't like me? I need you, I need you so much." Tears came again.

Later that morning five women from the village came to the house. They were dressed in black with a black veil over their face. Maheeba watched as they stood around the body, wailing, crying and thrashing about. "Why are you acting this way?" she thought. "You weren't my Ime's friends. You didn't even visit when she was sick. Are you the professional mourners Papa told me about? Do you really put onion juice in your eyes to make you cry?"

One of the women came over to Maheeba and tried to embrace her. She pulled away. "I swear I smell onions on you," she thought. "I don't like you people but I won't leave you alone with Ime."

The next day, Maheeba watched as they wrapped her mother in a black cloth, like they did in the time of Christ. Then she was laid on a stretcher. Tomas and Bashada, leading the funeral procession, carried their mother to her final resting place. Everyone chanted and prayed.

At the grave site, Father Yusuf prayed and the "mourners" in black threw themselves on the ground screaming and crying. Papa hugged his little children and they buried their heads in his arms. The body was lowered into a shallow grave and covered with dirt. A carved wooden plaque bearing her name *Madiam Bakeer*, would be the final reminder that she lived and died.

After the service, everyone returned to the house to eat, drink, and tell stories about Ime. Walking with his daughter, Papa stopped and sat on a rock. He took Maheeba's hand. "This is yours now. *Tata* gave it to your Ime and now I give it to you."

"It's Ime's relic. She wore it under her clothes. She kissed it all the time and put it under her pillow at night. I will wear it always. Is it really a piece of Jesus' cross?"

"It is what you want to believe."

"I miss her Papa. Where is she?"

"She is an angel now and can see you any time she wants. We can't see her. She is with us in spirit."

4

The grandmother I never knew, 1950

Mom told me that she took comfort in the thought that Ime could see her and she would talk to the spirit world often.

In the days, weeks and months after her mother's death, Mom felt Ime's presence during all the chores she did. The songs they sang while they were cooking, dancing in the kitchen, keeping time to the beat of a pan. She could hear her Ime say, "Don't forget to make a cross in the bread dough and say a prayer, that's what makes it rise." Mom had lost her best friend, her confidant. Who would help her make her wedding dress? There was nothing left but a well of memories, into which she would often plunge.

"If I close my eyes," Mom said, many times, "I can feel Ime's arms and legs wrapped around me, sitting on the ground, shelling peas so many years ago."

It was such a beautiful picture, my mother and grandmother together. I would beg her to tell me more.

"When I was a little girl," Mom said, "Ime taught me to sing this special song, *heck, heck betick ion,* like this, like this your house is clean."

Mom would relive this scenario through me. By the time I was three years old, she would stand me on the coffee table to sing *heck, heck.*

"Open your hands with your palms up, like you're giving a present," Mom said. "You make everything nice for your Papa. Now sway back and forth to show how clean your house is. Papa will be pleased. You make him proud."

I performed for my father and uncles. They gave me candy. Dad was so pleased that I became his special novelty act for all of his male friends. I was rewarded with trinkets. I soon learned to please the men was to gain praise and receive favors. It reinforced the desire to serve. Mom and my older sisters would dance for the men.

During the war, each time a brother or cousin came home on leave, the family had a big celebration. The men were served first, and entertained. The women waited for them to praise their culinary achievement. Then the children were seated. My mother and aunts ate leftovers.

I remember being with the women in the kitchen. They would giggle as they rehearsed a song or exotic dance for the men. They were happy entertainers, experiencing the thrill of performing for the perfect audience.

After the men had gone, and the women were cleaning up, they would light up a cigarette and pass it around. Mom held the cigarette between her thumb and first finger.

"This is sinful, but I like it," Mom said.

"Women in America do it all the time, and in public," Aunt Nadia said. "Your daughter, Marie, and my girls smoke."

"Yes, but they are not married to Syrian men," Mom said. "They don't smoke in front of their Papas."

The women ignored us children watching them, as they fanned the smoke out the back door with their apron.

My mother was my grandmother, personified. She was loving and kind, as long as the order of things was maintained. Women were to please and serve men. I enjoyed working with Mom in the kitchen. I liked to buy her things and fix her hair. There must have been a "thank you." I don't remember. But when I did something for my brothers, picking up their clothes, serving them dinner or relieving them from work, Mom would say, "You're a good Syrian girl."

5

Lady of the House, 1904

At the age of ten Maheeba was responsible for her father's house. Like Ime, her daily routine was the same. Get up, make breakfast, clean the house and then join the other women for the day's chores.

She would go to Hashar's house to help Confidad, and cook together. She enjoyed the daily visits because they would talk about the many widows who pursued Papa. Confidad called them the food brigade because each one would bring a special dish to impress Papa.

"Neldja, the widow, keeps coming to see Papa. Her boy fights with Farouk, and I have to take care of the baby. She is so mean and never smiles. Do you think Papa will marry her? I wish Ime were here."

"She is not so bad," Confidad said.

"I don't like her. Farouk doesn't either."

"I tell you true," Confidad said, "no one likes her, not even Papa."

"Honest?"

"Hashar say she wants to change everything. She won't last. Papa is set in his ways."

Maheeba noticed that her sister-in-law was cooking sugar and water. "Are you making candy?"

"Not to eat." When it was cool enough to handle, Confidad stretched it like taffy, working it back and forth.

"Let me pull some," Maheeba said.

"Put butter on your hands. You make candy."

As soon as Maheeba took a chunk of the sticky substance, she was transformed into a younger child, pulling taffy with her mother.

"We did this a lot. Me and Ime would pull and stretch, pull and stretch. I miss Ime. I hope Neldja doesn't come to the house anymore. There are lots of women after Papa. They bring food and sew for him. Some of them I like. Does he have to marry? Maybe, if I try real hard he'll be happy. I…what are you doing?"

Confidad spread some of the warm taffy on her upper lip. "I got mustache like Hashar." After a minute she pulled the mask off, exposing a lawn of black stubs. "Ime never did that."

"Your mother had face like angel. You should be so lucky. Take candy home to Farouk. I see you in the court yard, we work."

Some days Maheeba went to school with her brothers, Tomas and Bashada. Farouk stayed with Confidad.

According to custom she would walk behind them, just as she had when walking with her mother. Papa and the boys always walked about three feet ahead.

Often, Bashada would say, "Come little sister walk with us. Do you like school?"

"Yes, yes so much. I wish I could go to a classroom like you, learn to read and write."

"What for?" Bashada asked. "You have us to take care of you and some day you will get married. Don't you want to learn to cook and sew?"

"Yes, I want to be the best, just like Ime, but I want to read too."

"I'll ask Papa if I can teach you to read and write your name."

Maheeba smiled, "I would like that very much."

"You don't want to be too smart." Tomas teased. "Then no one will want to marry you. We will have to take care of you when you are old and fat."

When they arrived at school, Maheeba, with the other girls, went straight to the kitchen. This is where they would learn to cook, to sew, to serve. She even learned how to tell fortunes by reading the sediment in the coffee cup. As a result, Maheeba did not learn how to read and write, but she became a wonderful cook.

After school a few girl friends, Aida, Sarah, and Saleh would go home with Maheeba and help her to cook. They stuffed and rolled grape leaves, fixed eggplant or tried out a new recipe.

Maheeba mixed the meat and rice. Each one took a grape leaf, put the filling in the middle and rolled it up like a cigar. As they worked, they gossiped.

"My Ime wants me to marry Abdullah, and I think he likes me," Sarah said. "I like him. I'm working on a marriage gown. Saleh, what happened to your face?"

"I fell down, when we were grazing the sheep. I think Abdullah is cute."

"When will you get married," Aida asked?

"When I'm fourteen. He's only twenty."

"I don't know when I'll be able to marry," Saleh said. "My older sister is nineteen, and she isn't even spoken for. I'll probably be an old maid and take care of my father."

"This is my wedding dress." Maheeba showed them the white satin robe with gold embroidery down the front, that her mother had started sewing. "Confidad will help me finish it."

In a society where the life expectancy was forty to fifty, it wasn't unusual for a fourteen year old girl to marry. Most girls started planning early. Embroidering and all the little details took years to do by hand.

"Who will you marry?" Aida asked Maheeba.

"I don't know. Papa said he wants to be sure that the boy can make a good living. They talk a lot about America. Maybe I go to America. I hope my husband isn't old with lots of children. Let's make candy."

The girls boiled sugar water and made taffy. They pulled the sticky substance until it was light and airy. Then Maheeba rolled it into a log and sliced it.

When it was time for the girls to go, Saleh said, "You go on. I want to help Maheeba clean up." When they were alone, she said, "I really didn't fall down, my brother Saad hit me."

"What did you do?"

"I was helping him with the sheep and one of them fell into a ditch. I tried to get it out but his leg was stuck under a log."

"Where was Saad?"

"He was chasing the strays. Then two young Turks came by. One was mean and laughed. The other one helped me out of the ditch and carried the lamb. He seemed to comfort the scared lamb. I wouldn't look at him. He gently lifted my chin, looked me in the eye and said, 'You're pretty.' At first I couldn't say a word. I was scared. He was so handsome. His name is Jamal. Then we just started talking. I told him I would be in so much trouble if anyone saw us. He said he would too. You know that if a Muslim woman marries a Christian; their family has the right to kill her? I told Jamal he had to go and they left. It was too late, Saad saw us talking. He was so mad that he hit me hard and knocked me down. Then he kicked me."

"Didn't you tell him what happened, about the sheep?"

"He wouldn't listen. I grabbed his leg and begged him not to tell Papa. I was so scared."

"Did he tell?"

"No, thank Allah. You promise not to tell anyone?"

"You know I do," Maheeba said. "I'll never tell anyone as long as I live. You'll never see him again anyways."

"Maybe. He said he would be there Saturday and wanted me to meet him. He had kind eyes. I never knew a man like him."

"No, you crazy? I won't let you. You will get into so much trouble. Come to market with us. We'll have fun. You'll forget him," Maheeba insisted.

"I guess you're right. Do you think it's a sin? Should I go to confession?"

"We are supposed to love our enemies. I don't think you sinned."

"I better go now. I'll see you Saturday. What time," Saleh asked?

"Be at my house by six-thirty, or we will come and get you."

"Ok. See you tomorrow."

At the market place, Maheeba took Saleh to a stand where a man was selling fresh herbs. "See the bandages on his ears?" Maheeba asked. "Papa said the Turks cut off his ears because he was listening to a group of soldiers talking. They cut off a nose or hand for stealing. They could cut out your tongue for talking to that boy, if they thought he liked you."

"I'll never see him again. I promise," Saleh said.

One day a very pretty girl about, fifteen years old, came to the house.

"Sariya, what are you doing here?" Bashada, asked.

"My papa sent me with this gift. He wants to talk to your papa."

"Why?"

"I think he wants to arrange a marriage."

"He wants you to marry my father?"

"I don't know, maybe."

"Come in, sit down," Bashada said. "Papa, we have company."

Papa came into the room. "I am Mykhal, and you are the daughter of Hasish?"

"Yes. He sends you greetings and asks if you will come to visit. I bring you *Inkha,* cooked brains, I pray it pleases you."

"Thank you…," Papa tried to remember her name.

"Sariya."

"Yes. Tell your father I will see him after supper."

She bowed. As she was leaving, Maheeba arrived.

"Sariya, you come to visit?"

The two girls hugged, like old friends.

"I bring inkha with a special sauce for your papa. Good bye."

"I'll see you tomorrow." Turning to Papa, Maheeba asked, "She brought you a gift?"

"Yes. Hasish wants to talk. You like her?"

"She fixed my hair," Maheeba said. "We cook together. She is nice. I like her a lot." Going into the kitchen, she whispered, "Ime, maybe Papa will marry Sariya.

She is fun. She brushed my hair. When we shelled nuts, she showed me a trick. We sing when we work. It'll be like having a big sister."

"Papa," Bashada asked, does Hasish want you to marry his daughter? She is my age."

"We will see."

"I like her. Can I go with you?"

"Yes."

As she served dinner, Maheeba talked about Sariya. "She is a good cook. The inkha is better than I make, better than the teacher. She is pretty, almost as pretty as Ime. Don't you think so, Papa?"

"Yes, maybe."

After dinner, Papa and Bashada went to see Hasish.

"Welcome, come in. Sariya, bring the coffee and the baklava you made. We will smoke."

Sariya served the coffee and pastry. Grabbing her hand, Hasish said, "She is most beautiful, yes? She is the oldest and must marry first. She was promised to Gunta but a sickness took him. May he rest in peace. Now she has no husband. Mykhal, my friend you need a wife. She is a good worker, give you no trouble. I give you two cows."

"I am not ready to marry. Maybe…"

"I'll marry her," Bashada spoke up. "I've always liked her."

"I give you two goats."

"You said two cows."

"For Mykhal, maybe," Hasish said. "For you, two goats."

"Okay, first I want to build a house," Bashada said.

"My land will take care of my family," Mykhal added.

"Then I give two cows."

"It's a deal." Bashada held Hasish by the shoulders and kissed him on each cheek.

The next day Bashada went into the kitchen to see Maheeba. "How would you like to have Sariya as a sister-in-law?"

"Really? Who?"

"Me. When I build a house, you come visit."

"What about Papa?" Maheeba asked.

"He doesn't want to marry yet."

"I will like Sariya as a sister."

The next day, Sariya came to visit Maheeba, and they embraced and jumped up and down.

"Bashada is a good man, even if he is my brother. He reads to me all the time. Someday he will teach me to write my name. He likes his food hot and on time. He never tells me to wash his feet."

"I come to help you work," Sariya said.

"I have to wash clothes, everything is ready. You can carry that basket," Maheeba said as she positioned the other basket on her head.

Maheeba grabbed the bar of lye soap and they headed for the river. They climbed down the bank and joined the other women doing their laundry. She put all of the clothes into the water to soak. Then, one by one, she took each item out to rub with soap and scrub. Maheeba noticed her neighbor twisting the clothes and beating them against a rock. "What are you doing," Maheeba asked?

"You have to beat the water out. It will dry faster," she answered.

They gossiped and sang as they worked. After the clothes were washed, beaten, and lay out on rocks to dry, Maheeba and Sariya kicked off their sandals, pulled up their dresses and waded into the water. They splashed one another and giggled. The cool water felt good as they got soaked. Laughing like children, they stretched out to dry off. The older women shook their heads disapprovingly.

6

The contrast between Syrian and American women, 1949

Life for a girl in Syria was hard work, but emotionally simple and uncomplicated. There was no identity crisis. Her role was well defined—you marry and have children, accepting all the responsibilities for wife and mother. In my mother's family, it was an honorable position. If the boys gave her a hard time, Papa would chastise them "Remember," he would say, "That a woman brought you into this world." Once, he hit Tomas for being profane to his sister. There was security. Papa would tell his sons, "If anything happens to me, you must always take care of your sister. The farm will provide for all of you."

My mother accepted her role and was happy. "I liked pleasing my Papa and brothers," she would say. "It made me happy." She believed that men were godly and should make all the decisions, handle the money, smoke, and be promiscuous. She even believed that adultery did not apply to men the same way as women. After all, hadn't Allah taken the form of a man?

To an Arab woman it is a pleasure, a fulfillment, a reward to serve the men in their life. The gratification in being self sacrificial is analogous to serving God. Ime modeled her role well and my mother assumed the same responsibility.

Unlike most Arab women, my mother learned to write her name and read a few words. Her father believed that everyone should be able to read the Bible, but there wasn't enough time for her to learn. In America, she learned to read and write her name in English and a few words from the prayer book.

Although she had a burning desire to be literate, there was a limit as to how educated a girl should be. In America, Mom approved and even encouraged her daughters to attend school through the eighth grade. This was a privilege. "High school for girls," she said, "was excessive." The law provided for me and Ann to attend.

Being a descendent of an immigrant, I found myself between two cultures. I resisted being a Syrian, but I really wasn't an American. In 1949, when I wanted to attend college, my mother objected violently. "School away from home is dangerous. Women should stay home," she said. "You will get into trouble. Just get married. Let me die happy. You will give me a heart attack. I want to see you married before I die." She voiced her concern throughout my college career.

My father never objected and my brothers financed my education. I went on to higher learning. I was unaware of the duality of cultures until I went away to college. I felt inadequate, insecure, and different from the other girls. I was shy, with an inferior self image. They were outspoken, bold, and profane, demanding equal rights. It was shocking. However, they were respected and valued by their peers.

In a Social Studies class we were required to participate in a debate. "We have to debate Karl Marx's theory. Do you want to be pro or con?" asked a class mate.

"Neither," I said. "I'm not interested." What I really felt was afraid. Afraid to expose myself, to express my own ideas. It was safer to hide behind the shield of my brother's opinion.

"You have to be on the team for a grade."

"I'll be con," I said, "because the Catholic Church opposes Communism." I prayed for time to query my brother Paul.

I had no personal convictions. When asked for a political position, I found myself saying, "My brother thinks" or "my father said." As a second generation immigrant, I was emotionally crippled. Driven to make good grades, I was afraid to disappoint my brothers. The consequence probably would have been ridicule.

In college, I was counseled by Dr. Baron, my advisor, and discovered that I had the right to express my feelings. I became fortified with the freedom of speech and the armor of self worth. Slowly I grew more independent, creating internal conflict.

It was a culture within a culture. Being the good, subservient, Syrian daughter, was the role I played in the home. It was too painful to change. Being independent was risking disapproval, which translated into being a bad person. I liked the security and praise for doing what was expected of me. I could not stand the thought of rejection.

When I was home on weekends, I worked with my sisters at the Carlton, the family restaurant and bar. We worked during the dinner hour, so our brothers could go home for Mom to have dinner with all of her sons. The only time we all ate together was Sunday, when the business was closed.

I sympathized with the Arab women I knew. The only gratification they seemed to feel was in being submissive, unworthy and self-sacrificing. I once found myself opening a car door for my date. He thought it was a joke.

When I went away to school, men opened doors for me and pulled out my chair. It was a different world and at first it made me uncomfortable. In time I learned to like it. It felt good to be treated with respect; to be the recipient of attention, especially from a man.

One day, in 1951, I had come home on a weekend visit and was taking a shower. Just as I turned the water off, I could hear my brother Jimmy yelling, "Ellen, Ellen!"

Thinking the worst, I grabbed a robe, and ran to the kitchen. There was my brother calmly sitting at the table with knife and fork in hand. "I'm ready to eat," he said.

I was to serve him from the stove to the table. "Jimmy, go to Hell," I said as I walked out of the room.

"What did I say? What did I do?" he pleaded, following me up the steps?

Then I realized that he hadn't a clue. He too was a victim of another culture.

I sat on the steps with Jimmy beside me. "I was in the shower. I'm soaking wet. I thought you were hurt."

"Why didn't you tell me?" Jimmy said. "I would have served myself."

I could see the love in his eyes. I hugged him and thought, "You will have to walk on a bed of coals to find a wife in America."

I knew I could never fight my family or stand up to them. I knew that one day I would have to leave home. That day came, in 1952, when I graduated from college. With four of my sorority sisters we drove to California to attend a Gamma Phi Beta convention in Coronado.

"I'm not coming back," I said.

"What will your family say?" Jean asked.

"I'm not going to tell them. My mother would fake a heart attack."

"How are you going to pull that off? Where will you stay? What about your clothes? Money?"

"I have $1,700 saved, and an Aunt Anna who lives in Bakersfield. You will help me get my clothes out. Come over tomorrow and I'll give you a few things to hide. I can wear three blouses and pack as much as I can. If you will take three pairs of shoes, I think I can pull it off. My brother Paul is giving me $500 for the trip. We need to leave early so no one will be up."

"Are you sure?"

"Yes. I'll stay at the YWCA. I'll call my family. I know they won't like it."

We arrived at Coronado, and attended the convention. When it was over, the girls said good-bye to me in San Diego. Then reality set in. My first night at the Y was like staying in an opium den. The partition between the beds did not reach the ceiling. I looked up at the blue haze of smoke above my bed, and listened to the hacking and coughing from the women next door. I sprayed perfume around my bed to kill the odor of stale cigarettes. In the morning, I was nauseated from the smell of tobacco. I called Aunt Anna and Uncle Tom. By the time she answered, I was crying. "Aunt Anna, I'm in San Diego and I don't want to go home, but I'm frightened."

"Get the bus for Bakersfield; we'll pick you up at the station."

On my arrival, Lillie, Aunt Anna's daughter greeted me. "I haven't seen you for ten years. We've both changed."

Instantly, I was revived from the listlessness of heat and hunger. "I would never have recognized you," I said. "My big adventure away from home and I got scared."

"I think you're brave. If you want to stay in California, Cousin Rosemary is living in Hollywood. She came out a year ago with a girl friend and they live in a boarding house. We'll call her. Let's get you home. Mom has a million questions about relatives in Ohio."

I stayed with the Ryans for several days and then went to Hollywood to join Rosemary. As the days passed, I began to worry that my family would disown me. I wrote to say that I would not return to Ohio. No one answered my letter. A month passed; finally I called my brother Paul. "I don't want to go home," I cried. "Please understand, I can't lose my family."

"Stay as long as you want. We will always be here for you. It's okay to live in California, just come home for Christmas. I'll send you some money."

7

The Turks in Syria, 1906

Every month the Turks would come to collect taxes. They would ride through the village upsetting fruit baskets and let their horses stomp the contents to the ground. The terrified families stayed inside their houses with the door shut. As Maheeba watched them from her house, she saw Saleh looking out the window, watching Jamal with the tax collectors. Saleh's heart swelled with excitement. Jamal looked carefully at every house but never saw her.

"Get away from that window. You cause trouble," Saad said as he pulled his sister away. He carefully looked out and saw Jamal. "Why is he here? Is he looking for you? You want me to tell Papa?"

"No, I never saw him again. I don't know why he is here. I swear to Allah," Saleh pleaded.

Father Yusuf stood in the middle of the square. The soldiers rode around him with their swords drawn, jostling, trying to terrorize him. The priest never moved. He held out his hand with the tax money and a soldier grabbed it as he rode by.

Father signaled with a whistle for everyone to come out. "It is safe now," Papa said. "They are gone."

Saleh was the first one out of her house. She looked around to see if Jamal had gone too.

"Saleh," Jamal yelled as he rode back into the square. "Come with me."

She took a deep breath and held out her arms. Before she could say a word, he swooped down and swept her off her feet. They rode away, leaving the screaming villagers behind. Saad ran after them. Shaking his fist he screamed, "Come back, come back," Saleh never looked back.

"Father, you have to do something," Saad pleaded.

"There is nothing that can be done. I will speak to Murad, the representative to the Sultan. Prayer is our only hope."

"Papa what will happen to Saleh?" Maheeba cried. "Will the Turks kill her?"

"Maybe not. A Muslim man can marry a Christian woman, but a Muslim woman can never marry outside their religion, or they would kill her. A wife must serve the husband's God."

"Will Saleh have to become a Turk?" Maheeba asked.

"No, she will become a Muslim, and worship the Islamic Allah."

"Papa, why are they so mean?"

"Now, it is better," Papa said. They used to come every week. Many people died. The Turks would throw torches into the houses and run people down for the fun of it. They killed my papa."

"Why?" Maheeba asked in horror.

"He ran out to save a little baby goat. A Turk trampled my father with his horse, over and over. Then he chased the goat and stabbed it like a shish kebab. He ran the sword right through the heart and rode around waving the dead goat like a flag. I wanted to go help my father but Abraham pulled me back, and covered my mouth so I don't scream. I was little like you. When it was over, there were dead bodies and a river of blood. May they burn in Hell! Now they don't bother us so much."

"Papa was it always like this?"

"No, once Syria, Lebanon, Greece, Armenia, all the countries were Christian. This was the land of Jesus and the apostles. When the Turks came, they took slaves. Families were torn apart. Women were used in harems and as concubines. Some men were castrated to be eunuchs in the Palace. Men, not women, were given a choice to convert to Islam. If they did, they were freed. The Islamic religion spread by conquest. Now there are so many of them."

"Can they make us become Muslim?"

"No, Muhammad said you must convert by free will."

"It is so sad," Maheeba said. "How could Saleh even talk to a Turk.?"

"Some day maybe you go to America," Papa said. "It will be safer. No one tell you where to live or who to worship."

Epiphany, one of the most important holidays, is celebrated, twelve days after Christmas. It is the Feast of Purification, when Jesus was taken to the temple to be blessed and offered to God.

Four days before the festival, Maheeba woke up earlier than usual. "Ime," she thought, "today we make *zalabee,* doughnut cakes. I wish you were here to help me. It would be so much fun. It's my first Epiphany without you!"

The kitchen floor was clay, except for a five foot square wooden section with a trap door, which Maheeba lifted open. She climbed down the two rung ladder to the cellar where food was stored. She took out the small cross shaped dough which Ime had saved from the last batch of zalabee.

In a pan she mixed the flour, water and starter. I don't remember it being so sticky, she thought as she rubbed flour on her hands to smooth the ball of dough. She wrapped it in a white cloth, tied it and set it aside. Then she made coffee and fixed a breakfast of olives, cheese, jelly and bread.

"Coffee smells good." Papa said. "Do you know what day this is?"

"Yes, we 'baptize' the dough for zalabee."

"You have it already? You go with Confidad and take Farouk."

"Yes, soon."

Maheeba took the bundle, tied it to a stick and set out, a vagabond carrying her worldly goods. At Hashar's house, Confidad carried Mykhal and handed Farouk her bundle of dough. "Don't squeeze, just carry."

They walked to the well, where other women and children had gathered. A large bucket of water was placed on the ground. The ceremony for baptizing began with everyone chanting, *Be ism Il ab, Wal ibn, Wal Rooh, Il Kodos, Il tha-looth,* In the name of the Father, the Son, and the Holy Ghost, three in one. They immersed the dough into the water. The ritual was repeated for each house hold.

Completing the ceremony, they headed for home. "Remember to hang the dough in the tree for three days," Confidad said as she left the children. "I come on Friday, we fry zalabee."

"Why do we have to wait three days? Can't we have some today?" Farouk asked.

"We wait. The dough will rise without yeast. You'll see a miracle. I make some dough into a cross and save it for next time."

By noon, the village was bustling with women, sitting together preparing various foods. Maheeba, took her place with a wooden pestle and stone mortar.

"Let me show you how to crush wheat, it is hard work," one of her elders offered.

The air was filled with the smells of fresh mint, pungent garlic, fragrant cinnamon, parsley and sour lemons. The herbs and spices aromatically combined together to delight the senses. The women worked cooperatively. "I crush the wheat. You squeeze all the lemons," Confidad offered.

Lemons, used abundantly, were squeezed with one hand into the other, which served as a strainer. Maheeba learned, with other girls, how to hold the fingers close enough together to trap the seeds but let the juice run through.

By midday some farmer usually cut open a watermelon and called all the children in sight to share the treat. Always he would set a can in the middle of the circle of kids, hand them each a big slice of melon and challenge them to spit their seeds into the can. In this highly competitive society, children were encouraged to be the best: picker, runner, jumper, dancer, and seed spitter.

The women laughed, gossiped together and shared chores, but when it was time to cook, they went to their own homes. Behind closed doors, they prepared the food differently, adding a 'secret' ingredient or presenting it in a special way, so their food would be the best. Cooking, too, was competitive, and presenting the dish was a work of art. A hallmark of a good cook was to keep rice from sticking together; clumps of rice would be a disaster. Brown bits of *sharee'yee*, orzo, were added to the rice and lots of butter to coat and keep each kernel individual, like a grain of sand.

Syrian food was labor intense: crushing the *burghul*, wheat, with a mortar and pestle, then adding the meat and pounding again to make *kibbi*. *Koosa*, squash, was hollowed out and stuffed with meat and rice. Grape leaves were stuffed and rolled. Everything had to be made at home: butter, cheese, *laban*, or yogurt, jellies, pickles, wine and a drink, *arak*, made from fermented raisins or dates. Maheeba was taught to make everything, from *mezza*, appetizers, to an assortment of pastries.

A Christian Orthodox, she learned the religious significance of foods for Easter, festivals and weddings. There was an abundance of food and Maheeba took pride in cooking the same way her mother did.

She cooked and served the family as her mother had done, insisting that they eat more. If they refused even after the customary three-times offering, she would slip another helping onto their plate. Etiquette deemed that you refuse at least three times—accepting sooner would appear greedy. It was also considered polite for the hostess to insist, thus proving her sincerity.

"Maheeba, you made these cabbage rolls all by yourself?"

"Yes, Papa."

"Look how perfect they are, tight and firm, not loose and sloppy." Then he shot a stern glare at his sons to praise their sister.

Sometimes it was not so praiseworthy. Tomas screwed up his face, "The cabbage rolls are too salty," he complained as he reached for his wine.

Bashada, the peace maker, to the rescue, said, "It's not so bad with lots of bread and laban."

Maheeba walked over to her father for comfort. He held her hand open.

"Maybe this much salt, next time," he said as he drew a little circle in the palm of her hand. "We can add salt, not take it away."

Tomas tried to redeem himself. "I really love your *sfeehas*, little open face meat pies, the best I've ever had, like Ime's."

"Sit down with us. Eat," invited Papa. Maheeba and her mother rarely ate with the men. They ate in the kitchen or at the table as they cleaned up. Occasionally Ime sat at the table, with her arms crossed, like she was judging an eating contest. "Eat, eat, it will make you strong. It is good huh?" She would insist.

Sometimes Ime asked the boys what they would like for dinner the next day. "Just once I would like to request my favorite food," Maheeba said. Never, she was told, should a woman be assertive and ask for special consideration, even with food. It would be considered rude, bold, and brazen.

Maheeba sat at the table. Like Ime, she encouraged "Eat, eat," she smiled as she put another cabbage roll on Tomas's plate.

"Enough," he protested, but he was obliged to eat it.

"Maheeba, you must eat more, you are skinny. Put on some meat. People will think I don't feed you," Papa said. "Fat women are a sign of prosperity, but we don't want to be too prosperous."

After dinner, the men went into the main room and Papa lit the tobacco in the *narghileh*, the beautiful cut glass pipe with an oriental brass stem that cools the smoke by passing it through water. Maheeba enjoyed the sound of bubbling water and the incense like smell of sweet Persian tobacco. They would share by handing the mouthpiece on its long, cobra like flexible tube from one to another.

Maheeba remembered seeing Ime and Confidad smoking the narghileh in the kitchen, when no one was around. They would pass the pipe back and forth, giggling and trying to look sophisticated, and share information.

"The Russian Church make lots of trouble for the Turks," Confidad said. "Hashar say we go to war some day."

"Papa talks about more taxes on tobacco," Ime said. "The new Sultan blames it on the Christians."

When they were through they fanned the smoke so no one would suspect. "I wonder what Papa would say if he could see us now?" Ime asked.

"He probably knows, but never says nothing," Confidad said. "Don't you think he smells the smoke and wonders where the tobacco has gone?"

Every Saturday, in the summer, at dawn, Papa would go through the house ringing a bell like the town crier, "Get up, its market day."

Maheeba was tuned into the bell and would wake up smiling, "I love market day, when we pack up all of our fresh produce in the wagon and take it to town."

"Maheeba, make some coffee, Tomas, hitch the horses, Farouk help Bashada load up, yella, yella."

After breakfast she packed a big lunch for the day and handed the basket to Papa. Hashar drove. Papa, Confidad and the baby rode in the front, everyone else climbed in the back. They sang "Syria the Beautiful," and other folk songs for the two mile trip. When they arrived, they unhitched the horses and tied them in a grazing area. The men pulled the wagon into their usual spot at the open air market and began peddling their goods.

Maheeba and Farouk ran off to meet their week-end friends. "Maria," Maheeba called. "I'm so glad that you're here. I brought some palms, let's go make a crown."

"We don't have many Saturdays left. We'll make this the best day ever. What will you do in the winter?" Maria asked.

"When the dried apricots, dates and other stuff are ready, Papa puts them in baskets and sends them to Uncle Abraham in Damascus. I guess he sells them."

"Do you ever get to go?" Maria asked.

"Never, Elias delivers for most of the village. You ever go to Damascus?"

"No. We only trade here."

"Let's tell our fortunes, like we learned at school." Maheeba said.

"I don't go to school. Did you really learn how to tell fortunes?"

"I will teach you the secret," Maheeba said.

"I'll get some coffee," Maria said.

"After serving Turkish coffee," Maheeba began, "invert the cup, so that the sediment forms a pattern on the inside. Then turn the cup up and tell the future of your guest. See the 'legs' long lines? It means long life. The bits scattered around mean children or money."

"What if nothing sticks?"

"He will die," Maheeba said making the sign of the cross. "Ime told my fortune. She said that I will go to America."

8

My wedding, Los Angeles, 1952

In 1952, Pete Ryan, Aunt Anna's son graduated from Bakersfield High School and got a job in Los Angeles. Rosemary and I took Pete under our wing. He introduced me to his room mate, David Gray from Salem, Oregon. We were both twenty four, but from very different backgrounds. Dave was a conservative Anglo-Saxon Baptist, and I was a liberal Roman Catholic, Arab.

Despite my hesitation, I was charmed and dazzled by his intelligence and wit. To me he was good-looking, with his lean, angular physique. He was a gifted artist with strong convictions about the moral and ethical behavior of society. He was determined, opinionated and stubborn, much like my father.

I think that Dave was attracted to my seemingly adventurous spirit. He called me a 'pioneer,' leaving my family, and going out West alone. "I admire your determination to be your own person," he said.

I really was a coward, running away because I couldn't stand up to my family. I was physically free; no one could tell me what to do. But emotionally, my personality was still living in the shadow of my mother's culture. In time, Dave and I realized that I carried a lot of baggage. Maybe we thought that marriage would solve our problems. He proposed after five months.

We went to Portsmouth for the wedding. My family argued about the guest list, when, and where to be married. I was afraid my friends would not be invited. Even the date was a problem. It couldn't be on a week day, or Saturday, because it would hurt business. When I cried, Dave stood up to them and said, "If Ellen doesn't get her way, we will elope." I was so proud of him. I picked Monday, October twelve, Columbus Day, for the wedding. It was a holiday and the schools would be closed so my teacher friends could attend. My family's business associates would also be free.

My mother was so glad to see me married. "Now I die happy," she said. "I hope you have many boys, like me."

It was a beautiful wedding, but not a storybook marriage. We settled in Kennewick, Washington. With the money gifts, we bought a small one bedroom house. Unlike Dave, I had no talent for decorating, so he took over. Although we bought used furniture, Dave could not understand why I refused to buy anything without him. I made the curtains, but not without his approval.

We had three children. After the first two girls, I began lighting a candle for a boy. Although I resented the special treatment afforded my brothers, I was compelled to have a son. Mom would ask, "No boy yet?"

When I was pregnant with my third child, I called my mother. "This will be a boy," she said. "I pray for you." "Just like me, you will have two girls, five boys, and two girls."

Before my son was born, I saw visions of the Biblical king David, the slayer of giants. He was strong and determined, in Arab clothes. I knew that was the name my mother and grandmother had picked.

I found myself mimicking my mother and her values. It was uncomfortable at first for me to sit at the table with my family. My mother always stood and waited on us. She never sat down to eat until we had all finished. A rare occasion, I remember Mom joining us, she sat with her arms folded and said, "Eat, eat!"

As a wife, I put cream and sugar in my husband's coffee and stirred.

"What are you doing," he asked?

"I'm cooling your coffee, just like my mother," I laughed. I served him first and gave him the best. When I bought a porterhouse steak, I gave him the filet. The children and I ate the rest. I never satisfied my hunger until I knew that he and the children had enough. Dave did not like being treated in this special way. "Food should be divided equally," he said. "We spend the same amount of money on each other's clothes. Let me do things for myself. You don't need to wait on me."

I never bought a dress for myself or the girls without Dave's approval. I was inclined to buy the latest fashion which he thought was not prudent, such as a two-piece swimsuit.

Dave was not demonstrative, holding hands or kissing, which I interpreted as rejection. I was unhappy. I wanted his approval for everything.

In all fairness to Dave, my submissiveness was not to his liking. I failed him. He wanted a strong woman with convictions that agreed with his. We argued because I never complained. I was oblivious to the world situation: rising crime, drugs and the hippie movement. It didn't bother me. It wasn't enough that he complained about society's failures—he wanted me to join his crusade.

Once when we were driving and had to stop at a stop sign, he grumbled, "There wasn't a car in sight till I got here, now look, they're lined up."

It made me feel guilty, responsible for his discomfort. Why did he complain? Was it my fault? I was supposed to serve him and make him happy. I developed a twitch in my eye from stress. His cup was always half empty and mine was always half full.

When my son was enrolled in pre-school, I became a teacher. This allowed my husband to go back to school and get his Engineering degree. Working gave me self-confidence, because I was good at it. I continued my education and received a Master's degree in Pupil Personnel. I became more assertive which soon caused arguments.

The characteristics that attracted me to my husband were the ones I came to hate most. He wanted my opinion, but only to agree with his. He was a Republican and my family was staunchly Democratic, ranking Roosevelt right up there with Lincoln and Washington. I had no convictions. Rather than argue, I registered as a Republican. Dave saw the hippie movement as blight on society and I thought it was refreshing. He would not sit in a restaurant where there were "flower" children with long hair and beards. I bought a leather hair piece with a stick through it to contain a pony tail. When he saw it, he cut it up and threw it away. Dave nagged me about laughing too loud and not standing up straight.

After twenty-one years of counseling and therapy, we divorced. I felt that I had grown up at last and my mother had lost her power over me. It was 1973, and my mother was gone from this world, and I was free. That's what I thought and hoped for, but when I went back to Ohio, I found Mom's voice in my head as strong as if we were face to face.

I traveled alone, without my wedding ring. It wasn't long before my sister Ann noticed my ring less finger. "What is this?" she asked, holding my hand up. "You're, divorced?" Suddenly, I saw my mother, with one hand on her hip and pointing her finger with other. "An Arab, Catholic woman divorced." I might as well have been a street walker, I was doomed to Hell. There may have been bad marriages in my family, but there were no divorces, except for Marie. I cried. At least my tears gained sympathy from my siblings, besides they didn't care for Dave.

I returned to California, a new woman. It was as if the old me was looking at the new me and admiring how much I had changed. The old me was best described by a friend who called me selfless. I wasn't flattered. Little did she know how I was hurting? I needed to be special and independent. I didn't like being perceived as a caretaker, feeling responsible for everything. I couldn't indulge myself in simple pleasures. I didn't deserve a new dress that wasn't on sale nor could I eat the last piece of cake without knowing that no one else wanted it.

After the divorce, the new me bought a black sweater with silver threads and a fur collar. Dave would never have approved. I loved it. I joined a spa for meditation and exercise. I felt an aura of self confidence about me and it attracted men. I stepped aside for my date to open my door and pull out my chair. I taught school and supported my children. I continued my education, and received a Doctorate of Education. I felt confident enough to become an administrator.

But there were always parts of my personality I could not change. I was simply a care taker and needed to please others.

I hated my mother for not treating me as an equal to my brothers and not allowing me to express my feelings. I could not comfortably wear the curse of the Arab woman—approval from a man in order to merit love.

9

The Ottoman Empire, 1906

For 400 years Syria was a part of the Ottoman Turk's vast empire. Everywhere the Turks went there were religious and ethnic murders. The Ottoman authorities encouraged long-standing hatreds to spill over into massacres, with no regard for the sex or age of the slain. Stories of the "Terrible Turks" spread throughout Syria and the world.

By 1900 many Syrians were demanding independence. Influenced by Western ideas and the missionaries, Orthodox Christians began to cry for freedom.

Maheeba remembered well the night that the entire family was having dinner together, including Hashar and Confidad. Papa announced, "We have to talk."

"What is it?" Hashar asked. You seem so serious."

"I received a letter from our cousin Abdullah, in America." We will talk about it after dinner."

"Why don't you tell us about it now?" Tomas asked.

"One does not discuss money or bad news at the table—bad for the digestion," Hashar commented. "The letter must not be good."

Maheeba brought out a plate of hot *kibby*, and the aroma of lamb and butter filled the air.

"Did you make this?" Papa asked.

"Confidad helped me crush the wheat and meat, it's hard work using the pestle and mortar, but I made the meat and onion filling and baked it. I even cut it into diamond shapes," she said proudly.

Next came the baked eggplant, adding the smell of garlic and tomatoes, followed by rice and bread. The women served the men, poured wine and encouraged them to eat.

"Maheeba made the Syrian bread all by herself," Confidad said smiling. "A little thick, but very good."

After dinner Papa led the family into the sitting room. "Confidad and Maheeba, you come too."

"We have to clean up first," insisted Confidad.

"Leave it!"

Papa sat in his favorite chair and the others sat cross-legged on the floor. "Father Yusuf read the letter to me today. Bashada you read English, read."

Bashada took the letter. "He wrote in Arabic. Oh, the last part is in English." Looking it over, he commented, "Abdullah didn't write this, he must've had help, lots of help."

The beautifully written letter was read slowly and carefully, not to miss a word.

Greetings Mykhal,

I am writing to you with great concern. Your letter sounded so worried. Here the Turkish Empire is always in the news, predicting its collapse. Abdul the damned is called The Red Sultan, for the bloodshed he caused. British comic journals with "Punch and Judy" depict the ruthless Sultan as a cruel decrepit figure with a fez.

The League of Nations is demanding reforms. Great Britain is ready to fight the Ottomans. There is talk about the Syrians and other Arabs leading a revolt. Allah spare you. I don't know how safe you feel, but I am worried. Come to the United States, it is the land of freedom, where you can worship without paying a tax. I can sponsor all of you, promise jobs and provide a home. You must come, one at a time or all together. I have a big farm, about 100 acres. My children and I cannot handle it alone. I hire workers. I hire you.

Now I will write English. I study at night. My sons teach me. You must learn English. I speak good.

Allah be with you till we are together.

Cousin Albert

"I'm impressed," Bashada said, handing the letter back to Papa. "He changed his name to Albert. I don't remember him. How long has he been gone?"

"About fifteen years."

"What's a tax?" Maheeba asked.

"That's the Turks idea of freedom. Christians and Jews pay money so they can worship and not serve in the army."

"When do we go?" asked Tomas. "I think we are ready to drive the Turks out. If we stay we will fight."

"Yes, soon the time will come to fight the Turks," Papa said. "I have some money saved. We can start to plan your trip."

"I don't know if I want to go," said Bashada.

"That's because you have your eye on a certain girl." teased Tomas.

"We need you to go. You are the smartest." Papa insisted. "I think the three of you can go, later send for Sariya. Confidad and Mykhal can stay with us."

"No!" Hashar demanded, "My family goes with me."

"What about you, Papa?"

"I will never leave. I will be buried next to your Ime."

Maheeba walked over to her father, sat at his feet and leaned against his legs. "What will happen now?" she thought.

The months that followed were filled with planning, packing, and filling out forms. It was the talk of the village. "Go to Butalus, the tailor," Papa said. "He will make clothes for America."

The boys were fitted for suits, each one a different color with matching vests, white shirts and ties. For Confidad he made a long blue and white polka dot dress with a white lace collar and a belt. She had a long white headscarf, which she could wear as a stole. They had to buy shoes and socks to wear with their Western clothes.

"How are your brothers? When will they go?" asked a neighbor. "Maybe we should all go, like the Bible Exodus."

"Not everyone go?" Maheeba said. She had heard the older men vow never to leave their homeland. "Soon," she yelled back.

The final days, before the family set off for their venture to a new land, the entire village planned a feast. The women cooked for days, making meat pies, baked kibby, rolled grape leaves and pastries. The men roasted whole lambs and chickens.

Maheeba, walking through the village, could smell cinnamon, honey and sweet spices. From another house the aroma of lemon, garlic, and meat frying filled the air.

"Papa, Papa," Maheeba cried when she entered the house. "Everyone is cooking and getting ready for the big feast. It smells so good. I can hardly wait."

"Will you dance for us?"

"Yes. Sariya and me will sing, with a tambourine and everything. We are going to do the dance together with castanets and veils like Ime taught me. I'm going to wear Ime's snake bracelet." She danced around her father, twirling the dish towel over her head. "I'm going to sing "Syria the Beautiful" with Aida and Sarah. I wish Saleh were here. At the end, we will sing "America the Beautiful". I'm so happy; my brothers go to America and get rich. Is it really good luck to touch an American?"

"I don't know," Papa said. "If it is, this whole village will be lucky."

That evening a long white sheet was laid on the ground in front of the houses. The food was placed in the middle. The women held pans of water for the men to wash their hands before sitting on the ground. Men and boys ate first, then the children and women. Eating, singing and dancing lasted through the night. Maheeba remembered one other time for such an event, when a villager returned from America for a visit.

The day of departure arrived. The only man in the village with a truck would drive them into the city. Maheeba climbed in the flatbed with her brothers, Confidad and the baby rode in the cab with Papa. It was Maheeba's first trip to Damascus, Syria's cultural, economic, and political center. "That's the Barada River, which feeds our land," Bashada said.

"Where does it go?"

"It flows through the capital city and loses itself in a desert lake."

"Damascus is the oldest city in Syria and maybe the world." Papa told the children. "The Muslims say that when Muhammad arrived at the gates, he refused to enter, saying that, 'A man cannot enter paradise twice and the immortal one was worth waiting for.'"

"Did he ever see Damascus?"

"No. Like Moses he never entered the promised land."

Through the center of old Damascus cuts a street called Strait. "This is where St. Paul lived when he became a Christian," Papa said. They stopped at an open-air market to buy a few things. The crowded bazaar was pilled high with food, and spices. Maheeba looked at the silk scarves, woven from Eastern silk, wispy and light as air. The narrow, winding street was a contrast to the business district and signaled the beginning of a beautiful adventure.

For Maheeba and Farouk, it was a different world. People were dressed in beautiful Western clothes, of all colors. The women wore long dresses, tight at the waist, with shoulder pads and tight sleeves, white ruffled blouses and tight-buttoned jackets. Most of the women wore fancy hats with flowers or feathers and carried purses and umbrellas. Young boys had long pants with suspenders and long sleeved shirts.

In contrast, Maheeba wore sandals, a long green striped dress with sheer pants and a matching long green scarf. "I wonder what it's like wearing Western clothes," she thought. "Looks pretty but uncomfortable."

They saw tall buildings and the Great Mosque. "Is that a church, Papa?" Maheeba asked.

"It is a Muslim church," Papa said. "When the Turks came to Damascus and saw the beautiful Christian churches, especially the dome of the Resurrection, they were afraid. The Sultan said it had a 'seductive appearance'. He built the big beautiful Mosque with the gold dome to divert his people's attention. It was a smart thing to do."

A few college students, carrying signs ran passed Maheeba, pushing her out of their way. She could see the picture of the Sultan with an X across his face on one of the signs but could not read the words. "Why are they running, Papa?"

"Move out of the way." Papa said, as he pulled her towards him. "Look, the police chase them. They are protesters, trouble makers. They try to fight the Sultan."

Finally they arrived at Abraham's apartment in the Christian section of town, where they stayed.

"*Nishkor Allah wa-silt bil salami*, Praise the Lord you arrived safely," Abraham said.

After the preliminary greetings, kissing on both cheeks, comments were repeated. The children have grown, they said, and the adults look the same. "You have never seen our new apartment," Abraham said. "Life is a little better in Damascus. We still pay heavy taxes, and there is a curfew for Christians. Before we could not be in the streets after dark, but now we have until nine o'clock."

"This is very nice. May Allah continue to smile on you," Papa said.

Maheeba, with Farouk in hand, wandered around. "Such a beautiful place," Maheeba thought. The hardwood floors, the colorful upholstered furniture, so different from their plain wooden chairs. "Where do you get water?"

"From a sink. We have running water, right in the house."

"You don't have to go to the well?"

"That's not all," Bashada said. "They have an inside bathroom with flush toilets, and lights that turn on and off by pulling a chain."

Maheeba curiously admired the stove and shrieked when her *umtee*, aunt Nadima produced a flame by turning a knob and lighting a match. "Is it magic?"

"You silly girl," said Umtee, "it's gas."

After dinner, the children were treated to a trip downtown to see the lights and to eat ice cream. "I have to carry papers" Abraham said, "to show that we have permission to be out after dark. The streets get dangerous late at night."

It was a clear night. A warm breeze swirled around them, fanning Maheeba's scarf. The brick sidewalks were uneven and less forgiving than the dirt and sand of the village. The store's big glass windows displayed Western clothes. "Such big buildings," Maheeba said, "like a thick, cold, unfriendly forest." The bright lights lit up the town. There were so many confectioners shops filled with sweets.

"If you don't stop gawking, your head will twist right off," Papa said to his daughter."

"Amardeen," Maheeba said pressing her nose against the window and staring at the sheets of dried pressed apricots.

Uncle Abraham took them inside for a dish of ice cream. "I never had ice cream before," said Farouk. "It's so cold."

"I had it once," Maheeba said. "Chocolate is so good."

Papa bought a bag of Jordan almonds, to share. "We give these candies at weddings." It was a crunchy white sweet with a smooth coating of sugar over the core of almond. "It symbolizes a hard but sweet life," Papa said.

Maheeba held out her arms, like a helicopter, looked up and trilled around. "What a wonderful, magical world. Ime, I wish you could be here. Is America like this?"

"I hope so," responded Tomas.

Uncle Abraham gave the children each a candy bar. "This is a special treat, chocolate from Belgium, the very best."

"Can we eat it now?" Farouk asked.

"Not me," Maheeba said. "I'm saving mine to share with my best friend,"

"You have so little, why would you share?" Abraham asked.

"Then we can talk about it and remember. It will last longer. Once you gave me some chocolate and no one could understand how it tasted."

"Next time I will give you more, two, maybe three pieces."

Early the next morning, Nadima looked over the wall-to-wall sleeping bodies. She nudged the first one with her foot, "Yella, yella!" she said, then stepped over him and aroused the next one. "Maheeba, come with me."

Maheeba followed her aunt into the kitchen.

"My how you've grown, you're a pretty young lady. I haven't seen you since Ime died. You make coffee and get breakfast. There are olives, cheese, bread and hard-boiled eggs. I'll pack the lunch for the boys."

"The coffee is so dark," Maheeba said.

"It is real Turkish coffee. The only good thing they brought to Syria," Aunt Nadima said. We like our coffee hot and strong. It wakes us up."

Nadima filled a basket with little meat pies, cheese, fruits and other foods. She also packed a lunch for Mykhal, the children and the driver. By the time everyone got to the kitchen, everything was ready.

By mid morning they arrived at the dock. Maheeba thought she had seen everything, until now—a gigantic ship with four huge smoke stacks. An awe inspiring hulk. "It's big as a mountain, with little people. I never saw anything so big. It's all shiny white with a blue stripe and two flags flying. One is Turkish. Is the other American?"

"Yes," Abraham said, picking up Farouk and sitting him on his shoulders.

Maheeba made her way through the forest of people to the very end of the row. She could see everything. There were so many people walking up the gang plank while others were waving, blowing kisses and throwing streamers from the top deck. The loud fog horn blew. It didn't seem real. She tried to take in every little detail. "No one will believe me," she thought watching her family walk up the plank. They waved goodbye and then they were gone, swallowed up by the crowd. "Goodbye, goodbye, Allah be with you," Maheeba shouted.

She and Farouk tried to catch some of the streamers from the ship. "I want to remember everything, forever," she said, as she watched the anchor being raised. Maheeba held her ears as the ship's horn blasted its warning and slowly drifted out to sea.

As the children were pulled along, Maheeba kept looking back, watching the ship disappear into the ocean.

10

USA, the melting pot, 1940

From 1892 to 1954, over twelve million immigrants entered the United States. They were fleeing their homeland because of poverty, religious persecution or political unrest.

Portsmouth, like so many cities, became a melting pot of Poles, Hungarians, Italians and Jews. There were only a few Arab families, making us the minority of the minorities. The first generation of immigrants stayed together, trying to preserve their traditions. Theses people, who fled persecution and discrimination became very prejudiced. The oppressed became the oppressor. Everyone was a target, except the white Anglo-Saxon Protestant. There was no degrading name for Arabs because no one had ever heard of Syria. It wasn't until college that I was called a Camel Jockey. There were Spics, Dagos, Hunkies, Wops and Niggers. I probably chanted some of the rhymes without knowing what I was saying:

> If I'm a hunky, you're a Wop
> I eat chicken, you eat slop
>
> Ernie meanie minie mo
> Catch a Nigger by the toe

Although I was not teased, I sensed being different. There were condescending looks and snubbing by children of prominent families. I dated a student from Lindsey, a prestigious military school. Brian Caldwell was good looking and blond. His father was a dentist, and his mother was active in the Baptist women for civic pride club. He never invited me to his home and we avoided his relatives. Brian liked my mother. But his sister made it quite clear that she did not approve, and would tell his parents, if she saw us together. I didn't know if it was because I was Syrian, Catholic, or that my brothers were involved in gambling. Although we spoke English in the home, my father warned us that we had to prove ourselves because we were foreigners.

The Polish kid's lunches reeked of garlic. They had thick home made bread and salami sandwiches. Other students would walk by holding their noses. Kathy, my best friend and I would often sit with the outcasts.

Kathy was Syrian. Her beautiful mother was twenty-five years younger than her father.

"What do you have for lunch?" Martha Polaski asked me.

"Bologna on Wonder bread. I'm glad you can't make sandwiches out of Syrian bread."

"Want to trade?" Martha asked me.

"I don't like salami but you can have half of my sandwich for a slice of your bread." I loved the thick, white, homemade bread spread with butter.

Usually we had Mom's homemade jelly sandwiches or bologna. Sometimes we had "ham" salad made from bologna and occasionally peanut butter.

We had employed a black woman, Amy, for two years. She took care of my mother. She was a good cook, kind, warm and always singing. On Saturdays, she brought her daughter, Pearl who was my age, about ten. We played together, and could have been best friends, but I was told not to talk to a Negro in public, only nod.

One hot summer day I asked Pearl, "Can you go swimming with me, on the Island. My cousin will take us."

"I'll ask," she said. "Ma, can I go swim with Ellen and her cousin?"

"Heavens no, Chile. You know you ain't allowed on Saturday."

The public swimming pool was reserved for white children only. It was open to the blacks on Monday, and on Tuesday they changed the water.

"Why?" Pearl asked. "I'll be with white kids."

"You can't," her mother said. "That's the way it is."

"Can I go and watch?"

"If you want to stand in that hot sun. You behave."

Pearl stood with her nose pressed into the wire fence, on a very hot day watching us splashing in the water.

Even the Catholic Schools were segregated, "equal but separate". Once, when I was in High School, I was sent to deliver a message to Sister Paula at Blessed Martin's School, named after the patron Saint of the blacks. No one I knew had ever been in that school. It was out of bounds, forbidden territory, which made it eerie. There were no plants outside the fence, just gravel, in contrast to St. Joseph's flowering shrubs and grass. The playground was marked for games, like hopscotch, and four-square, but no basket ball court. I don't know what I was afraid of. Pearl was the only black person I knew, and I liked her. After her mother quit working, I never saw her again.

I walked inside the building. At the end of a long hall was a huge statue of the black saint, Blessed Martin. In the dark drab hallway, I noticed chipped paint and a crack in the wall. One classroom had a few students in uniform, seated at there desks. I made my way to the principal's office. "Sister Paula?" I asked. "I have a note from Sister Regina."

"Thank you," she said. "Are you alright?"

"Yes. I was afraid I would get lost."

"There's nothing to be afraid of," Sister said. "We are all God's children."

When desegregation was enforced, the restaurants, including the Carlton, displayed a set of dishes labeled "For Blacks." I was confused. Our housekeeper was a wonderful cook. I loved her, but I was still afraid that black people had a contagious disease.

In 1948 I attended my first year of college at the University of Alabama. When I arrived to register, I found that another student had requested my room, and I was to trade places. I thought nothing of it until that evening when a girl from Georgia came to me. "I was supposed to have that room," she said, "but I refused to stay with Doris, because she is a Jew."

I was oblivious to anti-Semitism. I didn't know any Jews. "Lucky for both of us," I said. Doris was very nice and I was determined to make her feel accepted. My nephew Joey invited us to a fraternity party. "Let's go and have fun. We will show those Georgia Peaches," I said.

Doris had to decline because we were Gentiles and would not be welcome in her home. "Gentile boys have only one reason for dating a Jewish girl," Doris said. We became very close roommates and distant friends.

In spite of our differences, or because of them, the United States has become a unique country. Our American heritage is made up of many, many cultures coming together to create a whole, greater than any individual part.

11

Maheeba's life without her brothers, 1906

"It's been two years since my brothers have gone to America," Maheeba said. "The village seems to be the same but the town is getting worse. Even children throw rocks at the soldiers. Christians aren't allowed in town after dark. We have to hurry home from church on Sunday. Father Yusuf talks a lot about war. He said the Turks have no money and they raise taxes. They put a tax on tobacco and blamed the Christians. I think Papa is scared. Every day I think about America. What's it like? Father Yusuf reads the letters to Papa and writes for him. They are fine. But Bashada got robbed once and beat up. Not everyone in America is good."

"Please Father Yusuf tell them to write about everything. What does their house look like, the furniture, the shops, everything." Maheeba begged. "I dream about that wonderful country with clothes and food shops and lots of sweets, like Damascus."

"I'll tell them you want to know everything." Father said.

After each letter arrived, Maheeba shared the news with her friends. "They don't get water from a well, it comes to their house, and everyone is rich and has a car. Some day I'm going to America, marry a rich Syrian and be happy forever."

"How can you go to America?"

"I don't know. Maybe Hashar will find me a husband and send him here to get me. We will have a big wedding and then go to America."

"You dream a lot." Aida said.

One morning Papa announced, "Mumduh, the butcher, is coming for dinner tomorrow. We will eat in the main room." Before leaving, he stopped at the doorway, as he did every day and kissed the feet of Jesus on the cross.

The main room, with the only rug in the house, was the living, sitting and formal dining room. That is where guests were entertained. It had no furniture except Papa's chair and a three foot high end table made of cedar wood, with an eighteen inch round bronze tray on top. That is where the men in the family went in the evening to smoke the *naghileh*, the water pipe.

Maheeba began to plan for the event in her mind. "I will cover the rug with a white sheet and put the tray in the middle. The food will be served in the big round communal platter, making it easy to visit and discuss business." She thought about the men eating in the traditional manner, sitting on the floor, without utensils. "The food must be eaten with the right hand, preferably with the first three fingers. How many times," she thought, "I watched Papa grasp a handful of rice, toss and squeeze it lightly into a ball, then pop it into his mouth without dropping a grain or touching fingers to lips. I can't do it. I want to lick my fingers. Ime could do it. What does it matter, I don't eat with the men."

She placed a bowl, a pitcher for water and a towel on the end table. She thought of the men ceremoniously washing their hands, each pouring for the other.

Maheeba went to Seloma and her daughter Aida's house to help make bread, to be shared with both families. The dough was ready. It had properly doubled in size and was divided into fifty balls. Each one took a ball of dough and rolled it as thin as possible. Following Seloma, the girls tossed it over the right arm, then the left in a swaying motion. With both hands balancing the dough, they twirled it in the air, over their heads. Each movement stretched the dough thinner, until it was three times larger than the initial size, about sixteen inches. The bread was quickly baked in a hot clay oven on one side and then with a wooden paddle turned over and baked on the other side. The tantalizing smell of fresh baked bread filled the air.

When the baking was completed, the young girls took the reserved dough, pulled off small pieces, rolled and stretched it into odd shapes and dropped it into hot oil. After it was fried, they slowly dribbled honey on their masterpiece and watched the sweet nectar disappear. They took their treat outside, found a shady spot, sat down and enjoyed the fruits of their labor.

"We are having company tomorrow," Maheeba said.

"I know. Do you know why Mumduh is visiting?" Aida asked.

"Business I guess."

"He wants to marry you. I heard my Ime talking to some of the ladies."

"He's old and ugly. It can't be true," Maheeba protested, "I'm too young."

"I'm promised to Naif *ibn*, son, of Khadra, someday."

"At least he isn't three times your age," Maheeba said getting up. "I'm going to talk to your Ime."

She went into the house and asked, "Do you know why Mumduh wants to talk to Papa?"

Seloma was dividing bread into two stacks and covered each with a cloth. "When I was getting some meat from him, he said you were growing into a beautiful lady. He asked if you were spoken for and I said I didn't think so. He said he would talk to your father. He's a rich man, good hearted and has no children. He's alone since his wife died."

"No! I'm going to America."

"Talk like that will get you into trouble."

Maheeba picked up her bread and put it on her head. She was so angry that she couldn't balance it without the support of her hand, and went home. On the way she mumbled to herself, "I know Seloma did that on purpose, telling Mumdah that I wasn't spoken for. She wanted him to marry me. Ime, I think she is trying to get even with you for marrying Papa. I wish you were here. You could tell her to mind her own business and ask Papa not to do this. I'm afraid. I dream of America. Please, Allah."

There was a lot of preparation for the night's dinner and for the next day but nothing seemed important now. All she could do was think, "Please Allah, don't let it be true." She cried, "Ime, I need you. You would understand and could talk Papa into anything".

Maheeba put her apron on and tried to plan her strategy. "How can I ask Papa what his intentions are without being defiant? I can't question him. Maybe if I ask permission. I could ask if he's buying some meat. I've got it. I'll tell Papa that Mumduh hasn't been to our house since Ime died. Is there a reason for his visit now?"

All afternoon, Maheeba's head was full of plans, over and over again. How to approach Papa in an acceptable manner? She was glad that Farouk was out with friends; she went about her chores, making lamb stew and rice. She would offer the green beans in tomato sauce, left over from the night before. For dessert, fruit, cheese and fried bread with honey.

By five o'clock Papa was home. She had a pan of warm water ready to bathe his feet. He came in and sat down on a kitchen chair. Maheeba presented the pan of water. He rinsed his hands and dried them with the towel his daughter carried over her shoulder. She then set the pan by his feet and took off his sandals. He slid his feet into the welcome bath. "You're a good daughter. Get me a drink of water."

When she returned with the water, she said, "How was your day. Are you tired?"

"Yes. Same as usual."

Maheeba swallowed hard and said, "Mumduh hasn't seen us since Ime died, may she rest in peace. Is there a special reason for the visit?"

"He wouldn't say, but I think you are the only thing that could interest him in this house."

Her dreams of America shattered. All the anxiety, the emotions she had damned up, exploded. "No! He's so old and ugly, I won't." The last word barely left her lips when she saw the fire in her father's eyes, and the muscles in his face contracting in anger.

"You dare raise your voice to me?"

Maheeba dropped to her knees and lowered her head waiting. Waiting for what? Would Allah strike a fatal blow? Papa to hit, he never did before. She remembered seeing lots of girls with bruises, but they never talked about it. She believed the guilt was theirs. "They must have done something bad to deserve it," Ime explained.

"I'm so sorry, Papa, I'm so sorry," Maheeba pleaded, crying. Her whole body shook with fear and anguish. "I'm sorry, forgive me. Please Papa, please." She grabbed the end of his robe and buried her face.

Papa patted her head gently. She looked up, tears streaming down her chin, "Forgive me."

He handed her his towel to wipe her face. "He is not so good looking. What kind of grandchildren would he give me? He's pompous and arrogant."

Maheeba felt her heart resume beating normally. "Oh, Papa," is all she could say.

His eyes softened, "You are beautiful like your Ime. Many men have asked for your hand, but I think you and Farouk go to America."

She wanted to make physical contact, touch his hand, hold it to her face but she was afraid to make the first move. Papa took one foot out of the water and shook it. Maheeba dried it and waited for the other one. She dusted his sandals and helped him put them on.

Then Farouk walked in. "Greetings everyone," he said.

"Get me a drink of water," Papa said, handing his cup to Farouk.

The next day was sunny and warm. Maheeba went out into the garden with Farouk to gather eggs and milk the goat. They picked some mint, tomatoes, and parsley for *tabbuli*, wheat salad. Farouk carried the eggs and milk. Maheeba put the vegetables in a shallow basket and carried it on her head. Not a master of this skill, she had to steady it with her hand.

After lunch Maheeba prepared for company. She took the *breek*, an earthen jug which had a narrow neck and wide base with a small spout for drinking, and went to the well. She filled it with fresh water. Holding the jug above her head, she let the water pour into her mouth, without touching the spout.

In the main room she filled the water pitcher, placed a sheet on the floor, and then started dinner. "Ime, I will make your favorite company dish," she thought, as she boiled chunks of lamb in seasoned broth. "It will cook for about two hours. I'll make sure it's tender and then I'll fix the rice while the men are visiting."

From the crock in the kitchen, she ladled some *arak*, strong liquor, into the pitcher. She and Papa had made it from dates, weeks ago. "What to wear?" she thought. "I would like to look ugly, paint my face and wear my old torn dirty dress, but Papa would get mad." She wore a plain black dress, which seemed appropriate for this sad occasion, and black leggings.

Papa came home early with fresh dates, apricots, and lemons. He tasted the *arak* to see if it had aged well. "A few more days and it will be better."

"Do you want to wash your feet?" Maheeba asked.

"Not today, I don't feel good. I'm going to lie down. Get me a drink of water."

Maheeba returned to her chores. "I will make a dinner most festive, like Ime," she thought as she lined a deep platter with Syrian bread, making sure the ends hung over the sides, so the men could tear off a piece. "I'll spread the seasoned rice over the bottom with chunks of lamb piled on top. Just before serving, I'll pour the sauce of seasoned butter over the meat. I'll sprinkle pine nuts and parsley on top, for my special touch. Ime, are you watching?"

At the appointed hour, Mumduh arrived. Farouk answered the door and greeted him "*Alan wa shlan,*" welcome to our home.

When Mumduh saw Maheeba he handed her a large package. "It is a quarter of a lamb, the hind quarter, the best part and there is something extra special, sweet breads."

Maheeba took the gift and thanked him.

Papa came to greet his guest. The two men went into the main room. The children went into the kitchen.

"Take this," Maheeba said, handing the package to Farouk. "We have to put it in cold storage." She lifted the trap door in the floor, at the far end of the room, exposing the cellar. Farouk climbed down the short ladder and put the meat into a wooden storage box.

"Help me take in the *maza,* appetizers," she said, handing Farouk a plate of hard-boiled eggs, cut into quarters. She then delivered dishes of sliced cucumber, tomatoes, radishes, olives, cheese and lamb tongue salad, to round out the appetizers.

Farouk saw Maheeba hiding behind the wall, trying to hear what the men were saying. "Shhhh!" she said holding her finger to her lips. They walked into the kitchen. "Here take this plate of dates to Papa and listen to what they are talking about. They stop talking whenever I walk in."

Farouk took the treat into the main room and put it in front of the men; he sat back on his heels and listened.

"Eat," Papa said. Farouk helped himself.

"He is growing into a handsome man. Here try the *arak,*" Mumduh said, offering his glass to Farouk.

"No, thank you." Farouk refused three times, and then Papa nodded his head, yes. Farouk took a sip of the strong liquor and coughed. The men laughed.

"You will soon be a man," Mumduh said.

"Go tell Maheeba we are ready to eat," Papa said.

When Farouk got to the kitchen, Maheeba asked, "What did they say?"

"I think Mumduh likes you. He was saying nice things about you. He said you were pretty and could cook. He wants someone who can give him children."

"I wish I had burned the dinner and had warts on my face," thought Maheeba. She took the main course in and placed it in front of the two men.

"This is beautiful, you cooked it yourself?" Mumduh asked.

"I can't cook everything, I'm not so good. Seloma helps me a lot." She looked at him. Tomato dripped on his shaggy beard and he talked with his mouth full of cheese. He touched her hand and she stiffened. She tried to study Papa's eyes, Was he giving in? The evening lasted an eternity. After coffee and dessert, Mumduh inverted his cup, and asked Maheeba to tell his fortune.

Maheeba knelt down, picked up the cup and looked at the residue of coffee. "You will have a long life and prosper."

"Will I marry and have children?"

"Yes, I see a beautiful widow with lots of children in your life."

Smiling, Papa lit the *narghileh* and passed the pipe to his guest. Maheeba went back into the kitchen until he was gone.

Maheeba was still cleaning up when Papa came into the kitchen. "I told him you were too young," Papa said. "He wanted to wait for you, a couple more years. I told him you and Farouk go to America."

Maheeba's eyes lit up. "Thank you, Papa. Ime, I'm going to America, your dream for me will come true!"

"You happy? Papa asked. "You don't want to marry a Syrian boy and stay here?"

"I don't want to leave you, Papa. Come to the new world. We'll make a happy life."

"This is my country. I'll die here. You go. War is coming soon. They will raise the taxes again."

"Hashar said there are lots of Syrian men in America. Maybe he will find one for me."

12

Easter in Syria, 1907

The next day, Papa said, "Make the sweet breads tonight, it is special."

"I don't remember ever having them before," she thought as she unwrapped the package. She looked at the strange contents. "Not like meat, it was white and soft, like brains but not the same. I don't know how to cook this stuff. I'll go ask Seloma."

She took the package of sweet breads next door and asked, "How do you cook this thing?"

"This is a delicacy. Don't cook long. You fry some garlic in oil then add the sweet breads. Cook maybe ten minutes, then crush garlic with salt, just a little, and add some lemon, put it on top. Sometimes they eat it with eggs. Scramble some eggs on the side; your Papa can eat them together if he wants. It will be delicious."

When Papa came home, Maheeba shared Seloma's recipe for sweet breads.

"It sounds just right. You cook in half hour, I lay down first"

Maheeba served the dish with the pride of an accomplished chef. It was golden brown with a delicate aroma of garlic.

"Umm, it's wonderful." Papa pressed his three fingers to his lips and blew a kiss. He put some on Farouk's plate.

"It tastes funny, I don't like it."

"Eat the eggs and rice."

"I'm glad Farouk doesn't like it, maybe he'll leave it for me," Maheeba thought. "I really want to try it. I wish Papa would give me a taste." As much as he loved his daughter, it never occurred to him to offer her a bite and she would never ask.

"Where do sweet breads come from? I've never seen them before."

Papa grabbed his throat, in a dramatic gesture. "He has to be a big bull to get a good meal."

As soon as Papa left the table, Maheeba picked up Farouk's plate and took a bite of the succulent treat. It was so delicious, she licked the plate.

The next day Maheeba was thinking how strange it was not having her older brothers at home. Her chores were lightened, less cooking and cleaning. She now realized that the boys consumed enormous amounts of food and created tons of dirty laundry. Life was definitely easier.

Papa, Farouk, and Maheeba were closer now. She thought, "like the Trinity—the Father, the Son and I'm the Holy Ghost."

Early Sunday morning, they headed for church. Spring was coming. The Pomegranates were small, not quite ready to eat. Maheeba packed a few dried apricots for the journey. She noticed Papa putting water in the sheepskin vessel, usually reserved for trips longer than the one mile they would travel today. Papa had been drinking a lot of water lately and his stomach pains were more frequent.

They arrived at church early. Papa lit a candle for Ime, then took the lit candle and held it under his chin. Maheeba could smell the singed hair. The few seconds he held it there seemed like an hour. "I proved my faith," he said as he carefully placed the candle back into its holder in front of the Statue of the Christ child.

"Do it again Papa?" Farouk asked.

Without answering him, Papa led the children to their seats for Mass. By the time they arrived back home, Papa had drunk the whole half-gallon of water.

It was Easter week, and the following Saturday, the children gathered root vegetables, beets and onions to dye the hard-boiled eggs. Farouk was so excited. "Can we dye some brown eggs too?" he asked.

Ime would boil onionskins to give the light brown color, and the henna dye from the leaves of the camphor tree would provide a deeper brownish red hue.

"Maybe," Maheeba said. "But we have to take red eggs—signifying the blood of Christ—to the church to be blessed by the priest."

Maheeba boiled beets, a brighter red than pomegranate skins, and added the eggs to cook and dye at the same time. She also boiled an additional six eggs for them to color.

Farouk watched the pot. A half hour later, the eggs were ready and Maheeba took them out to cool. She took a candle and said, "Look what I learned in school." After making a cross of wax on a white egg, she dipped it into the henna dye. When she retrieved it, there was a beautiful white cross against a reddish brown background.

"Let me try," Farouk said.

Maheeba went to get a basket to put the eggs in. While she was gone, Farouk took an uncooked egg and hid it under his folded hands.

When she returned, he innocently asked, "Can we eat one of the eggs?"

"Okay, but not till noon, when Lent ends."

"Can I break an egg on your head?" Farouk asked.

"No, that's silly. You'll get shells all over my hair."

"No I won't. Please, you can break one on mine first."

"Alright," Maheeba said, giving in to childish pranks. Reluctantly she picked up a white egg and cracked it broadside on Farouk's head. It was funny and the shell held together.

He laughed, "Now it's my turn." He picked up the raw egg and crushed it on his sister's head, the slimy yolk and clear substance streamed down her face.

"Farouk, wait till Papa gets home!"

"I'm sorry," he laughed as he picked off the bits of eggshell from her head. "I didn't know it would make such a mess."

Her first impulse was to get even but that would make another mess for her to clean up. Farouk continued to wipe up the drippings on the table, while Maheeba went outside with a pitcher of water to wash off her hair.

"I'm really sorry, honest," Farouk said. "I didn't think it would make such a mess but it was funny. You're always fixing up your hair and you never let me get dirty. Do you want to break a raw egg on my head?"

She looked at her little brother. "No, and I won't tell Papa." They both laughed.

On Easter Sunday they dressed in their best church clothes. Farouk wore a white and black plaid short sleeved *abeyal*, a cloak, over a plain white long shirt and a white *hatla*. The head scarf was held in place with an *akal*, a head coil wrapped in fine black silk with a gold ornament in front. Papa wore his blue and white striped cotton cloak and white silk head scarf with a black silk head coil decorated with blue and white beads. Maheeba wore a pale red robe and Ime's long white silk headscarf. She walked up to Papa for approval.

He smiled lovingly. "Beautiful, like Ime, but something is missing." Papa opened his hands to present Ime's gold, coiled snake bracelet with fiery ruby eyes.

"My favorite thing, the slave bracelet. Thank you," Maheeba said as she dropped her scarf and rolled up her sleeve. It was too loose. "Papa make it fit."

Fitting it around his daughter's upper arm, "It is solid gold, it should bend easy."

She ran to the mirror.

"Why do they call it a slave bracelet?" Farouk asked.

"Long time ago, in the Bible, when God's people were made slaves in Egypt, they had to wear a metal arm band with the mark of the family who owned them. They could never take it off. Men wore them too."

Maheeba returned, hugged her father's arm and closed her eyes. "I will wear it always. It will be good luck." Then she put the best four red eggs in a basket, including one for the priest. Papa filled the sheepskin vessel with water.

They each touched the cross as they walked out the door and headed for church.

During the service the congregation, carrying lit candles, followed the priest. They paraded around the inside of the church three times, stopping at the back door. A man, representing Satan, stood in the dark behind the closed door to prevent the priest, representing Christ, from entering.

The priest chanted, three times, for the door to be opened so the King of Heaven may enter. On the third chant Satan vanished. The priest threw open the door to symbolize the victory of Christ over Satan.

The church was immediately illuminated and the people began to sing, "Christ has risen." At the end of the service, the eggs were blessed and distributed by the priest. The congregation greeted each other by hitting their eggs together, symbolic of breaking fast since eggs were forbidden during lent.

The children challenged each other to an egg fight, hitting the opponent's egg at the top and then the other end. If the egg broke, they were out of the game. The winner, with the surviving egg, showed it to the priest and was rewarded with another egg.

As Papa greeted Father Yusuf, he mentioned that he was not well and would the priest tell his sons in the next letter to America.

The family started home. Papa drank a lot of water and had to rest several times.

A month earlier, word came that Bashada would be returning home from America. They would plan a big feast, but Papa would never see his son.

"Let's have a fire tonight and cook shish kebab, (lamb on a skewer). Farouk, you gather wood for the fire."

Papa placed two metal tripods on opposite sides of the fire pit, to cradle the long skewer. He lit the wood to a blazing fire. Maheeba brought out the seasoned chunks of lamb, onions, bell peppers, a platter of rice, Syrian bread, and a small pitcher of *Arak* for Papa, and a pitcher of thin, liquid yogurt for drinking. Papa skewered the meat and vegetables, and placed them on the tripod to roast.

When the meat was cooked, he took a piece of bread and slid the succulent chunks onto the rice. They ate from a common bowl. The three of them sat around the open fire, watching the flames barely fluttering on this windless night.

Farouk looked at his sister and said, "Tell the story about Snef Snef, the dog, like Ime used to."

"Snef Snef was a rich, arrogant, selfish, dog who never helped anyone," Maheeba began. "He saw a hurt dog sitting in the road, who cried, 'Help me, help me' but Snef Snef said, 'I can't be bothered.' He was so vain that when he got to the well he stood on the rim and looked at his reflection in the water. He leaned over to see more of himself and fell in. He cried, 'Help me, help me.' Everyone who stopped looked in and said, 'I can't be bothered.' 'Help me please before I drown.' Finally the dog who was hurt dragged himself up to the well and looked in, when he saw Snef Snef; he said, 'Grab my tail.' Snef Snef tried to jump up but he couldn't reach it. The hurt dog crawled over to the bucket, tied it to the rope and dropped it down the well. Snef Snef took hold and—"

Maheeba's voice trailed off, as she looked through the flame and saw Papa take another drink of arak, close his eyes and fall to the ground. His right arm landed in the flame, catching fire. Maheeba screamed and pulled Papa away. His arm was burning. She threw dirt on his arm as fast as she could to extinguish the fire. Farouk helped.

"Go get *Hunna,* quickly!" Maheeba ordered her brother. "Papa, Papa, can you hear me?" She blew the dirt off of her father's arm, put his head on her lap and rocked back and forth praying. The smell of burnt flesh and singed hair conjured a fearful picture. She picked up his purplish black arm, the color of eggplant, it was still hot. The flesh fell open; exposing the bone and his fingertips had turned to ashes. He was unconscious. She stared at the red flame shooting sparks, ready to devour everything in its path. "Please Allah," she cried.

When Hunna and Seloma arrived, they wrapped Papa in a blanket and carried him into the house. Maheeba, kneeling on the ground, held her head with both hands and cried. Between sobs she repeated, "Oh Allah, Allah, Allah." She stood up in a daze and looked at her dress, covered with dirt and soot. Farouk hugged his sister and they held onto each other.

They went into the house and just stood there holding each other while the adults took over. Seloma put a wet cloth on Papa's forehead. Hunna went to get Elias and the truck to take Papa to the Clinic.

The doctor had to amputate Papa's arm. He had diabetes, and never recovered from surgery. Friends and neighbors took care of the children until their uncle Abraham and aunt Nadima arrived from Damascus.

The funeral was arranged. The professional mourners wailed, cried, and threw their bodies on the grave. Papa was laid to rest next to his beloved wife. Following the burial the house was open for mourners to come in to eat, drink, and tell beautiful stories about the deceased. Mumdah was very kind and he provided most of the meat for the woman to prepare. At thirteen, Maheeba felt she had lived a lifetime.

A few days later, Bashada arrived. He comforted and loved his two siblings. "It would have been different in America. Papa would have been treated for diabetes."

They stayed together for a month, the proper time for mourning. Bashada entertained the children with stories of the Western World; the people, food, clothing stores, sweet shops and music. "They call me Charles, in English."

He then arranged for them to go to America. "I'm not going back with you, maybe some day, but now I want to stay in Syria with Sariya. You'll be all right, I have the necessary papers. Our brothers will sponsor you and I'll give you twenty-five dollars."

He then told of the long, boring trip. "Sometimes it was interesting and exciting. I made new friends with the same hope of a new life. There were so many people from different countries. Everyone was friendly. They sang and danced in their own customs. You will enjoy the trip and you will like America; it is your dream. If they have a hard time spelling Maheeba, tell them your name is Mabel or Melba, they will probably call you May. It's better to pick your own name. Farouk, you will be Frank. Here I wrote it down in English."

"Mabel, it is a good English name, I like it." Maheeba walked away studying the spelling.

The day they were to leave, Bashada took down the cross that hung by the front door. He wrapped it in a towel and handed it to his sister. "Take this with you. It will give you a part of our homeland and our customs."

"It is Papa's cross. I love it, thank you. I will keep it with Ime's relic." Maheeba held them to her chest and hugged her brother. "They will always be with us."

They spent a few extra days in Damascus, so the children could get Western clothes and prepare for their big adventure. They had to be immunized and get passports. Maheeba wore her mother's gold bracelet on her arm, under her blouse, and carried the cross in her hand.

The family took the children to the big ship. "My arm hurts," Farouk said to Maheeba. Why did they do that?"

"So we won't get sick. Mine hurts too. The doctor put all five shots in one arm. It will get better soon."

While waiting to board, Abraham made friends with a Syrian couple, the Nadars. He paid them to watch out for the children. "Maheeba, Farouk! Meet Mr. and Mrs. Nadar, they are passengers too."

Bashada gave the children a last hug and handed them a package of streamers. The Nadars each took a child's hand. They walked up the lower ramp to the third class deck. The children looked over their shoulder and waved good-bye. Once on board, they tried to make their way to the railing. A few adults stepped back to allow the children to stand in front. Mr. Nadar lifted Farouk up to throw his streamers.

Maheeba grabbed the railing and pulled herself up and stood on a protruding bolt. Balancing on one foot, she threw her streamers over board. Passengers were waving and shouting to their loved ones. "I love you."

"Good sailing," Bashada called out.

"Allah be with you," Maheeba shouted back as they sped away to the roar of the engines.

Maheeba and Farouk quietly watched the dock disappear. They stood there as though they were waiting for their family, who would never reappear.

13

At sea, 1907

"Children, Children!" Mrs. Nadar called, and they followed her voice to the third class recreation area. Maheeba listened to the hum of the engine, as they made their way to the dormitory like cabin which slept six. There were cots to sleep on; the toilets and sinks were down the hall. The newly formed family settled in their cabin. Maheeba and Farouk had two suitcases of clothing and a basket of food, which they deposited on their bunk.

They looked prosperous compared to some of the passengers with boxes and cloth bags. "So many of them already look tired and weary before we even set sail," Maheeba said, as she passed by the older men and women. She followed a Slavic woman carrying a bag on her back, to her cabin. She watched the woman undo her bundle and pull out a feather bed. The lady noticing Maheeba motioned for her to come in.

"It's beautiful," Maheeba said as she caressed the fluffy material and held it to her face.

The old woman smiled, nodding her head with approval.

Maheeba made friends with their room mates, Joseph Haljin, age ten, and his Mother Sera. They were from Aleppo, in northwestern Syria. He spoke Syrian, although he was Armenian. "We escape massacre," Joseph said. "I was only five but I remember. One day my mother see the Turks coming and she put my cousin's dress on me and a scarf on my head. I don't understand. Then the soldiers came in with my father. They made us all line up against the wall. I stand next to my mother. My Uncle and an old friend came from the cellar with their hands up and the soldier just shot them. My Uncle say 'Allah' and die. The soldier opened the gate and all the soldiers came in with women, children and boys from other farms. We sit on the floor and lean on each other. There was no place to lie down. The next day they take all the boys, my Aunt's four children and my father and go. See my mother was smart, they think I'm a girl. One soldier stayed at the front door to guard us. My mother go to him and say, "I leave my daughter

64

here and go fetch some bread. I'll bring you some." He agreed. She came back to me and say, "When I leave, you go out the back way and run. He's not going to leave the door and chase you." My mother went out, and I ran fast as I could. I looked around and see he's not chasing me. My mother grabbed me and we ran to her cousin's house, where there were only women. Every day I look out the window and see them line up the men and shoot them. They would rape the women, tear off their clothes, but I didn't know what they were doing."

"How did you get away?" Maheeba asked.

"My mother got friendly with a Syrian soldier. He had to serve in the Turkish army and they were mean to him. He hated the Turks and was glad that he was getting discharged. He made two square boxes, one for me and one for my mother. He draped them over the horse. The soldier wore his uniform and gun. The horse had the Turkish insignia. No one stopped us. He took us from Bitlis to Aleppo, where we lived for five years and I had to go to a terrible Arab school. Now we go to America."

"My brothers are in America and they send for us," Maheeba said.

On board, the passengers, mostly men sporting a variety of fashioned beards and sharp moustaches, were hoping to prepare the way for their families. The Italians, Irish, Russian Jews, Romanians and Greeks were the largest groups, and only twenty Arabs. They gravitated to their own kinsmen. Maheeba noticed men in kilts, Englishmen in short knickers, and other Arabs in long robes. Everyone was excited and in a festive mood, smiling, shaking hands and nodding to each other.

Farouk quickly found friends. Even though they didn't speak the same language, they could share their toys. Farouk showed off his wooden carved animals, wagons and figures. His prize was the catapult on an axle, which shot wooden balls by tapping the opposite end of the seesaw. He and the other boys enjoyed roaming around the ship, and helping the sailors with their chores. There were a few children Maheeba's age. Everyone tried to practice English and communicated with single words and gestures.

There was a small kitchen on the same deck, where food was dispensed. For the first week the food was substantial, soups and stews for dinner. For lunch there were sandwiches, cheese, fruit, and a brownish liquid they called coffee. The breakfast fare was hearty with lots of eggs. For the children, it was an adventure in Western foods: pancakes, cereal, and sandwiches. By the second week there was less variety and less food. The bread became hard. Maheeba would dip the bread into water to soften it. There was always fish mostly herring. It was supposed to help prevent seasickness.

A Slavic girl sitting next to Maheeba had never seen white bread before. "You eat?" she asked.

"Yes," Maheeba nodded. "It didn't kill these other people. It must be safe, and I like it."

"If you don't eat all your food, save it. We might need it later," Mrs. Nadar told the children.

In the evening everyone would gather in the common quarters. They would sit in a circle, on boxes and luggage, and tell stories of their homeland in animated broken English. The men who brought instruments: harmonica, tambourine, accordion, lute and a guitar, would play for different groups to sing and dance their folk songs.

Dominic, from Italy, played his accordion and sang. Maheeba and Farouk sat down to watch and listen, as the slender, curly haired, middle aged man, closed his eyes and serenaded the other passengers.

Farouk noticed his sister looking solemn with tears in her eyes. "What's the matter?" he asked. "What is he singing?"

"I don't know. It sounds so sad. I think he is telling about his beautiful village and all the friends he left behind. The family he will never see again. He's probably remembering the old country that holds his past and wondering about the new world that holds his future."

"Are you scared?" Farouk asked.

"Sometimes," Maheeba answered.

When the song ended, the tambourines began to sound. "Ump a." A Greek lady, snapping her fingers shouted, "We dance!"

A Greek boy grabbed Maheeba. They locked arms; side stepped, and hopped. Once around the circle, and then they turned their heads and changed directions. Maheeba discovered that the *dubkee*, was very much like the Greek line dance and she readily joined in.

The ocean, a vast expanse of gray, restless water, seemed to go on forever. Unlike the Ghuta River, it was not calm, and there was no land in sight. "America must be way out there somewhere," Maheeba thought as she watched a shark jump out of the water and dive back in. "I wonder what kind of fish that was. There are so many big ones."

After ten days at sea, they encountered a storm. The water was extremely rough. Mrs. Nadar and many other passengers got seasick and were confined to their beds. Some just lay on the floor for days, groaning, crying, and throwing up.

With hot water and lye soap, those who had the strength, tried to keep everything clean, but the stench of sickness remained. Many people were sick, a few died. They were taken to the doctor's quarters and never seen again. The reality of life seemed cruel to Maheeba. It was a cold world, where only the fittest would survive.

Every three days two women from first class would visit. They would bring a basket of left over food from their table, and some sweets which were given to the sick and the children. "I would like to know these elegant ladies," Maheeba thought. "They must be very kind and rich. They are so beautiful in their long dresses with capes and gloves."

An elderly Slovak woman with dark, sunken eyes and hollow cheeks would take the basket and distribute the food to the needy. She always wore a scarf, *babushka*, and a toothless grin. She noticed Maheeba admiring the women. "Much money," the old woman said, as though she knew what Maheeba was thinking.

"I help," Maheeba said, as she took food from the basket and handed it to a little girl who was following her.

Farouk made friends with an eleven year old Jewish boy named Jacob. "Maheeba come meet my friend."

"Where you from?" She struggled with her English.

"Russia. They come to kill us. My Papa say, 'We give you food and liquor.' They drink, no kill us. We run away at night," Jacob said.

"You run from Turks?" Maheeba asked.

Jacob looked puzzled, "Cossacks."

"They Muslims?"

"No," Jacob answered. "Orthodox Church, pogrom."

Maheeba could not understand why the Christians would fight the Jews.

As the days went by, she spent more and more time on deck. There were no deck chairs. Wrapped in a blanket, she would sit on the floor, dreaming and praying. "Allah," she would pray. "Let America be a wonderful place. No terrible Turks to scare us. Ime make my dream come true. Give me a rich husband and lots of sons." Sometimes she felt a little homesick but never wanted to go back. Maheeba liked to feel the wind in her face and watch the angry water beat against the ship. Some days the first class passengers would look down. They always seemed friendly and would throw food or candy.

Even more than the dreams, she enjoyed listening to the music at night, from the forbidden deck above. The beautiful sounds filled the night air with magic. Maheeba could imagine the women in evening gowns with long gloves and capes, like those she had seen in the shop windows in Damascus. They would be dancing to the beautiful sounds of the orchestra. She pictured the ballroom with gold and mosaic walls like the Mosque. It would have the Sultan's chairs of red velvet with high backs and a gold crest.

There must be flowers and beautiful dishes with lots of sweets. These wonderful moments would make the boring days in close quarters bearable.

Sometimes, Farouk would join her fantasy. "I wonder what the dance is like?" she said as she grabbed Farouk's hand. "Come dance with me." They put an arm on each others shoulder and swayed back and forth. Then Maheeba closed her eyes and twirled around and around to the tune of a waltz. Farouk would laugh and she would pretend that he was her handsome, rich husband. When the music ended, Maheeba opened her eyes and there she was with her little brother. She felt suspended between two worlds.

14

Ellis Island, 1907

After eighteen days at sea, the ship arrived at New York harbor. The children stood side by side on the deck, lost in their own thoughts as the pea-soup fog slowly unveiled the giant lady holding a torch against a bright blue sky background.

"Look! Look at the statue. Is it a Saint?" Farouk asked.

"I don't know."

"That is the famous Statue of Liberty, America's promise of freedom. It is a gift from France," Mr. Nadar explained.

Maheeba looked at all the people on the dock, waving at the passengers. She was first struck by the sight of American men without beards. In contrast to her countrymen, they looked pale. Men in Western suits looked more important, more impatient and everyone wore a hat. She saw her first black man, a porter carrying bags.

It didn't take long for Maheeba to realize that she was a world away from her quiet, peaceful village. She knew this the moment the ship docked and she saw the high rise buildings and felt the excitement of action packed New York.

"There are so many people," Maheeba said. "How will our brothers find us?"

The first and second-class passengers were processed on board and disembarked to the cheering crowd. Maheeba, Farouk, the Nadars and all the passengers in third or steerage class were ferried to Ellis Island.

"Where are we going?" Maheeba asked Mr. Nadar.

"Ellis Island is where they will ask us questions and give us a medical examination."

"What kind of questions?"

"Do you have a sponsor, someone to take care of you? Yes, your brothers. Show them the letter. You have to have at least twenty-five dollars and be healthy. Then the ferry will take us all to Manhattan, to meet our families."

The day they arrived at Ellis Island, in the spring of 1908, over ten thousand immigrants were processed. Maheeba looked up at the Main Building, the palatial red-brick structure. "It's a palace," she thought. "An American immigrant palace." The awesome sight of this enormous building was inspiring; a new home, a new life, freedom from the Turks. It was so big and strange, it was intimidating. She held the cross close to her, and at times rubbed the bracelet on her arm. The two children walked to the iron railing and looked across the Atlantic towards the Manhattan skyline. So many buildings, standing together like a concrete family of odd shaped members.

"This is America, Farouk, smell the seawater and look at the birds."

They watched the chirping seagulls swoop down to get food. The fog had lifted, leaving the sun to warm the earth. It was a beautiful day.

"Maheeba, children, this way." The familiar voice of their friends, the Nadars, called through the crowd.

Maheeba tucked Farouk's white long sleeved shirt into his gray pants, straightened his suspenders and dusted off his tweed jacket. He wore Western clothes. She wore her best native outfit, a navy blue dress-robe with little yellow flowers, blue billowy pants and a long matching head cover.

"This way. We have to register." The Nadars led them into the enormous hall.

"There are so many soldiers," Maheeba said. "Like Damascus."

"You are to separate," a female nurse said. "The women will follow me, and the men go with him." She pointed to a male attendant.

"I don't want to leave you." Farouk said, holding onto his sister.

"Go with Mr. Nadar," Maheeba said. "You can't come with the women. I'll see you later. It will be alright. We are in America."

They were taken into a large dressing room and handed a blanket. "Take off your clothes and give them to the attendant," the Nurse said.

Maheeba held the blanket to her chest, resisting the embarrassment of undressing in public.

"We have to do what we are told," Mrs. Nadar said. "We are all women. Just wrap the blanket around you."

It was the first time Maheeba saw a naked woman. The attendant took their clothes to fumigate and delouse. Then the ladies had to take a shower with a disinfectant soap. "It smells terrible," Maheeba thought.

After the shower, she wrapped herself in the blanket. It was so warm and comfortable. When she got her clothes back, they were wrinkled. She noticed one lady crying, because her threadbare dress was torn. Maheeba dressed and went to Mrs. Nadar.

"Why they do this?"

"They don't want us to bring germs or bugs from the ship," Mrs. Nadar said. Then they were led into the Great Hall with iron railings dividing the rows of people. They took their place in line and waited for an hour to be examined. "It is like the Tower of Babel," Maheeba said, looking at the confused people who were speaking a variety of languages, she couldn't understand. There were hundreds of interpreters speaking thirty different languages, but that was not enough to serve the Babel of tongues.

Maheeba watched a doctor with a large piece of chalk examine each person. "What is that?" she asked, when the doctor branded a man with an 'E'.

"He has bad eyes, he may be sent back. The H is for heart and the Pg is for pregnancy," Mrs. Nadar said.

"They can send you back?" Maheeba said, looking at others branded with an X for retardation. She was getting nervous and afraid. She kissed the cross and rubbed her bracelet. "Allah will protect us and maybe the snake will ward off evil spirits," she prayed.

The Nadars went first. They were approved and waited on the side for the children.

Maheeba stepped up to the doctor and he checked her heart, her ears and she walked for him. With a long metal buttonhook he rolled back her eyelid to check for trachoma. Maheeba froze, trying not to act frightened in front of Farouk. "Are you pregnant?" He looked up and said, "Of course not."

"What is your name and how old are you?"

"Ma…Mabel Bakeer, and I'm thirteen."

"Who is this young man?"

"My brother."

"What is your name?"

"Farouk or Frank Bakeer and I'm eight years old."

"Where are your parents?"

Maheeba just shook her head.

"Your mother and father?"

"They are dead. May they rest in peace?" Maheeba made the sign of the cross.

"What are these kids doing here?" He shouted to another administrator. "Get them out of here!"

Hearing this, the Nadars walked away.

"No!" Maheeba protested. "We go to America!"

"This way kids," a man in a white jacket said as he pulled them out of the line and led them to a screened room with benches. "In the cage," he said, as he opened the door and closed it behind them.

They looked at the men sitting there, branded with an X. The children sat down. Maheeba, holding her cross to her chest, began to cry hysterically. The indignity of being processed, her hopes and dreams shattered, was more than she could bear. What would they go back to? She reached for her handkerchief as a hand touched her shoulder. She opened her eyes and saw a pair of beautiful, shiny, black and white shoes with clean gray spats. Her eyes followed the well-creased pants up to a shirt, tie, vest and jacket. He was handsome with a small mustache. He handed her a handkerchief.

"Are you a doctor?"

"No, my name is Nicolas Thomas. I saw you getting off of the Ferry and I was behind you in line. I'm from Beirut, Lebanon." He said in Arabic.

"They want to send us back to Syria. They won't listen. My brothers are waiting for us, and I have twenty five dollars. Why do they do this?"

"In our country, you are a woman at thirteen but in America you are a minor. Children with no parents."

"Hashar is papa now," Maheeba said, beginning to cry again. "Don't let them send us back, please. I dream about America."

"Can you help us?" Farouk asked. "My brothers will pay you."

"Maybe, if we were married, not really, just pretend. You could get in as my wife."

"What about Farouk? I won't leave him."

"I will say he is my responsibility. They allow families in together and I have good sponsors."

"Let's give it a try. Point out the doctor who examined you and we won't go to him."

"I thought it would be like heaven," Maheeba said.

"Yes, but Saint Peter's been replaced by an examiner."

They walked to the other side of the building and got in line. "He is so handsome and nice," Maheeba thought. "I wouldn't mind if we did get married."

They waited another hour for their turn.

"Tell them my American name is Mabel."

Nicolas walked up confidently to the doctor. "Here are my papers and this is my family."

After the usual questions, the doctor asked, "Do you have your marriage certificate?"

"Yes, it is in Arabic but you can see from the Cross on the paper that we were married in the church."

He looked at Maheeba, such a pretty young girl. "Okay, I guess everything is in order."

They were given their papers with the seal of approval.

"You did it, but you lied to the official." Maheeba said.

"A white lie maybe. Let's celebrate. I'll take you to a movie."

"What's a movie?" asked Farouk.

"You've never been to a movie picture show?"

"No."

"I've been here since last night. I know my way around. They have some shops and a theater. It is a self-contained island. There's a playground on the roof. I'll give you a tour. First let's have lunch. We'll talk, get to know each other, then go to the movies."

It was time for lunch, so they went to the dining room. There were long rows of tables with benches, enough to seat 1,200 people.

"There is so much food," Maheeba said. "It is the land of plenty. Do we have to pay for it?"

"No," Nicolas said. "See that sign over there? It says 'No charge for food.'"

They were given soup, a meat or peanut butter sandwich, fruit, and coffee or milk.

"I'm hungry. What is this?" Farouk asked.

"Peanut butter and jelly," Nicolas said. "You like Western food?"

"Most of it, but the rice looked like mashed potatoes. Not like Maheeba's. On the ship we had lots of fish."

Looking at Nicolas, Maheeba said, "My brothers will appreciate what you did, but you're Lebanese, they won't like that."

"In America, it doesn't matter. We are all Arabs here."

"Do the Lebanese hate Syrians?"

"In Lebanon they do."

"Why?"

"We are a small country and a long time ago, Lebanon was once a part of Syria, but under the Turks we developed our own trade and became economically strong. We want to be our own country. We don't like to be called Syrians, we are Lebanese. Most Syrians I meet, I like. I like you," answered Nicolas.

"I like you too, and I know that Maheeba likes you."

Maheeba blushed, "Farouk!"

"Why did you have a marriage certificate?" Maheeba asked. "Are you married?"

"Yes, but my wife is sick and could not come with me. She has a bad cough. They would never let her in. I hope, later when she is well, I can send for her. I need the certificate to get her in."

"Your name is Nicolas Thomas?"

"It is now. I tried to tell the ships registrar in Arabic, *Nicolas ebin Tomas*. They didn't understand, so I said I am Nicolas son of Tomas. Nicolas Thomas he wrote on the ships manifest. I don't argue. I met another Arab family, they had a tag on their son, to NY—to New York, and the registrar wrote Tony. I wonder if he will change his name."

Maheeba was confused, "Tony wasn't his name?"

"No, maybe it's not so funny. To NY happens to spell T o n y."

"Have you been to America before?" Maheeba asked.

"No, but in Beirut I worked for a dry goods company, we shipped material, and things to New York. I have friends there who make and sell clothes. They are my sponsors."

After lunch they walked to the theater. The cowboy movie had just begun. Nicolas paid for the three of them and they walked into the dark room. Their eyes had to adjust. Farouk stared at the screen. It was like real life; horses running, the riders coming right at him. Some one was reading the sub-titles "don't shoot! Don't shoot!" The cowboy pulled out a gun and aimed it right at the audience "Duck!" Farouk shouted as he pulled his sister to the floor. "He's going to shoot."

They heard the words, "Bang! Bang!" Farouk and Maheeba looked up and the horses were leaving. Nicolas helped the children up and led them to a seat. They were mesmerized throughout the movie.

"Can we see it again?" Farouk begged.

"I guess so, if they don't throw us out."

So they sat through the second showing. It was late when they left.

"Have you seen movies before?"

"Yes, Beirut is a big seaport, with tall buildings and stores, like Damascus but smaller," Nicolas said. "We'll catch the Ferry tomorrow morning. After dinner I'll show you the sleeping quarters. Men sleep across the hall from the women, so Farouk will stay with me, Maheeba, you will sleep with the women."

The food was substantial: meat stew, boiled vegetables, bread, fruit, cookies and milk or coffee.

"What is that?" Farouk asked, pointing to a strange yellow thing on his plate.

"A banana," Nicolas said. "It's a fruit. You peel it and eat."

"I don't like it. It's too soft."

After dinner they headed for their sleeping quarters in another building. They said good night and parted.

"Be good and listen to Nicolas," Maheeba said taking Farouk's hand. "Don't talk to much. I'll see you in the morning."

Maheeba walked into the room and stopped at the sight of triple-tiered bunks. There were so many women: Italians, Greeks, Jews, Poles, and others. So many languages, she had never heard before.

Mrs. Nadar came up to her, "I'm sorry but my husband would not let me get involved. There was nothing we could do. Will you go back?"

"No, there's a friend who helped us." Maheeba walked away.

"I'm glad for you," Mrs. Nadar called.

There were hooks on the wall for coats. Another room had toilet stalls. In the middle of the bath room were ten sinks facing each other. Maheeba, used the facilities, then found an empty bottom bunk and started to climb in, when she heard a child crying. "There's lots of crying in this place," Maheeba mumbled, as she stood on her toes to look into the bunk above. She saw a fair skinned little girl about Farouk's age. Maheeba smiled as she brushed the child's black hair from her face. Without exchanging a word the two children knew they shared the same fear of being separated from their family.

"Pointing to herself, she said, "Maheeba."

"Helena," the little girl said, as she pointed to her eye and drew an invisible E on her dress.

"You?" Maheeba asked.

"No," the child shook her head. "Nick."

"Your Papa?"

"No."

Maheeba motioned to Mrs. Nadar for help.

Just as Mrs. Nadar came over Helena's mother appeared.

The two older women talked. Then Mrs. Nadar sat down with Maheeba on her bed.

"The family is Greek," Mrs. Nadar said. The son, Nick, has something wrong with his eyes, maybe a sty. You know children get them all the time. His papa said, 'The family stays together.' If the boy is sent back, they all go. The doctor took him away to try to cure it. We pray for them. Go to sleep now."

"Good night." Maheeba took off her robe; long pants and head cover, folded them carefully and set them on the foot of the bed. She decided to sleep in her undergarment. "This is a frightening place," Maheeba whispered. She kissed her cross, and slipped it under her pillow. She climbed under the blanket, put her head down and thought over all the events of the day. She dreamed about Nicolas—even if he was married, even if he was Lebanese.

The next day they joined the human tide of immigrants. As they walked down the Staircase of Separation to the boat, Maheeba heard someone calling her name.

"Maheeba, Maheeba!" Helena called as she pointed to her brother Nick, and smiled.

Maheeba waved, "Allah is with you." Turning to Nicolas, she said, "That is Helena, her brother must be well. They won't have to go back."

The Ferry docked at Manhattan where Tomas was waiting. They hugged. He kissed Farouk on both cheeks and looked at Nicolas.

"This is Nicolas Thomas and this is my brother Tomas," Maheeba said.

Holding out his hand to shake, "Call me Tom."

"He adopted us," Farouk interrupted.

"If it weren't for Nicolas, I don't know what would have happened to us. The doctor would not let us come here. He said we were too young. We were scared, I cried."

"That's why they call it the 'Isle of Tears,'" Nicolas remarked.

"Thank you very much. We are obligated to you," Tom said as he shook Nicolas's hand. "If there is ever anything we can do."

"Please allow your sister to write to me. I would like to know how everything turns out for her. We are just friends. I am married."

"In that case, here is our address. We live in Ohio." Tom handed him a card.

"Thank you. I see my friends. I must go. I hope Farouk gets to see another movie soon. Good bye."

Tom turned to the children, "We'll have to hurry to catch the train," he said, hailing a cab. Each of them grabbed a suitcase, Tom carried two, and handed Maheeba his picnic basket. They climbed in and headed for the train depot.

"Wow," Farouk said, "we get to ride a train."

Maheeba, walking behind Farouk and Tomas, boarded the train last. She looked at the rows of beautiful red velvet seats, like the fire in the snake's eyes. She sat next to a well-dressed lady, across the aisle from her brothers. Tom deposited the luggage overhead and under the seat. Maheeba handed him the basket "Are you hungry? I have sandwiches, cheese, fruit and some candy."

"Candy," Farouk echoed, "can we have some now?"

Maheeba sat back and thought, "Ime, I'm in America."

15

Ellis Island the museum, 1995

My mother made a voyage not only across the sea, but also across time. It was a journey from Syria and a way of life that had not changed for hundreds of years to America that was changing too rapidly to define its culture. I asked my mother how she felt when she landed on the Island. She said, "My first impression was like standing at the foot of the Tower of Babel; everyone was confused and speaking a different language. No one knew what to do or where to go. No one smiled. I was scared."

I wanted to experience vicariously what my mother felt, and I was determined to make the pilgrimage alone.

Ellis Island is the landmark of America's immigrant heritage. From 1892 to 1954, more than twelve million people—third class passengers on steam ships, were processed to enter the United States. It was the largest mass of human migration in the history of the world. Their descendants, including me, account for more than forty percent of the population, of the United States. Walt Whitman called New York, the "City of the World," because all races, from every continent were represented here. After a massive restoration project, the immigration depot was dedicated as a Museum in 1992.

I visited this historic site in 1995. Leaving my friends in New York, I took the Miss New Jersey Ferry, and purchased a senior round trip ticket for eight dollars. It was a beautiful, warm sunny day, and the breeze mussed my hair. On deck, I had to hold on to the railing to steady myself. There were two enclosed levels with tables and benches, and a snack bar. I enjoyed cookies and coffee on the way, a luxury not afforded the immigrants of 1908. Most of them were transported in an open barge.

After passing Miss Liberty, the turreted brick of Ellis Island's receiving station became visible. I closed my eyes and tried to imagine my mother and uncle, staring at the palatial red-brick structure that architect Robert Twombly describes as "designed to intimidate while it inspired." I wondered if it had a trace of the infernal about it, because the only palace my family had ever seen was the Turkish Sultan's.

Our ferry docked and we immediately disembarked. If the immigrants were lucky, they only had to wait for thirty to sixty minutes before stepping on the pier. Their boat load was kept together, and they were identified by individual numbers. From there, I walked the fifty feet to the building, picturing the people struggling with their luggage. My mother described an old lady carrying an enormous bundle on her head. "She just stood there for hours," Mom said. "It was all her worldly possessions."

I walked up the long stairway to the Great Hall of judgment. "The doctors must have watched the immigrants walk up the stairs to see if they limped," I thought. The room was two hundred feet long and fifty-six feet high. Here the immigrants were evaluated as potential Americans.

From photographs, taken in 1980, and from written documents, I was able to reconstruct my mother's dilemma. In the Registry Room, mom, thirteen years old, would have seen a maze of bars, high wire pens, walkways and locked gates, along with uniformed guards and inspectors. Most evident would have been the doctors and nurses in white uniforms who performed the medical examination. The physical test was designed to screen out those destined for welfare or harboring infectious diseases. As many as two percent of the people were sent back to their homeland. On a record day in 1907, 11,747 immigrants were processed. Every two minutes someone was approved or detained.

The law required that a child be accompanied by an adult, in case he or she was rejected by the examiners. If the child had to return to the country of origin an adult was required to journey back with them to their homeland. I thought about large families, if a child were rejected, one adult would have escorted him back and perhaps never to see the rest of the family again.

My mother must have been terrified at the prospect. In reality, if she passed the test, she and Uncle Frank would have been detained on the Island until their brother claimed them. But fate played a more exciting hand, and my father came to her rescue.

In 1911, three years after my mother arrived, benches replaced the iron railings so the weary could rest as they waited for hours in line. The dining room served 1,200 people with diverse tastes. There was a separate kosher kitchen maintained for the Jews. Mom and Uncle Frank had their first banana and peanut butter sandwich on the Island. I was raised on these two favorites.

The hospital had rows of wooden beds with thin mattresses. There was a Chapel with wooden benches and a plain Alter with a cross above it. These echoed the history of births and deaths. One could live and die on this self-contained island world.

I had to see the theater where my family saw their first movie. It was renovated with plush seats and lighting. I recalled Uncle Frank's story, "I was sure the cowboys were going to shoot us, so I pushed Maheeba out of the way." I have great memories of him taking us to see every cowboy movie that came to town and peanut butter sandwiches for lunch. Memories of the past were preserved on film. A picture of the kitchen and its equipment covered with plaster from a deteriorating ceiling was taken in 1982. A small picture of a saint, a hair comb with most of its teeth missing, a rusted spoon and fork, a broken toy, and portraits, all formed a still life of the past. As many as three thousand people at a time were housed there. Their graffiti read like poetry, "When your fate is to pass from here, you will pass." A Polish immigrant wrote, "I come to America *sa chlebem,* for bread."

I walked to the other side to look across the water at Manhattan. The landscape was dominated by the Twin Towers, standing like giants. My mother saw many tall buildings, but she would not have seen this famous and tragic landmark, nor will my children. The Towers, like the immigrant palace, are now in the archives of history.

16

Settling in Portsmouth, 1907

After many hours of travel they arrived at their destination; the rest of the family was there to meet them. Maheeba hugged Confidad and picked up Michael and kissed him. "You are so big, and heavy. I haven't seen you for three years." He just smiled.

They all climbed into the green Nash. Farouk sat in front, between his brothers. "Is this your car Hashar?"

"It's our family car. We live together and we work together too."

"Are you married?" Maheeba asked Tom.

"No, someday I will go to Syria and get a wife. I'm saving my money." They pulled up to a big brick house.

"We live here." Hashar said.

"It's beautiful. Just like my dream," Maheeba said.

Portsmouth was a small town of three hundred, mostly Polish immigrants. Unlike her little village, it had big houses built of wood or brick, with basements and barns. Some houses even had a garage.

In the fall Maheeba remembered her village and the agreeable scent of fruits drying: mint, lemons, and grapes. In Portsmouth these sweet smells were replaced with the pungent scent of cabbage fermenting and garlic for salami. "What is the smell?"

"Sauerkraut and sausage," Tom said.

"What is sauerkraut?"

"It is cabbage that they cut up and put in crocks with salt. Like pickled turnips," Tom said. "They cook it with pork. It's sour. I rinse it off, and add sugar. I like it. New Year's Eve, it is good luck to have sauerkraut and sausage."

This was one of the few new foods that Maheeba did not like, but otherwise, she enjoyed life in America. Settling down in Ohio, her chores were much lighter, and she found time to visit with friends. Maheeba checked the mail every day. Finally the long awaited letter arrived. She took the envelope and ran to her friend's house. Panting, she knocked on the door then walked in. "Rose, here, read this to me and don't leave out a word."

My dear friend, Maheeba,

I hope that America is everything you wanted it to be. As for me I am doing well, working in a dry goods store and saving my money. My wife is not well. I am afraid it is worse than she says. Pray for her my friend. Tell me about yourself and Farouk. Are you working?

I think of Farouk every time I go to the picture show. I am staying with friends for now but I am looking for an apartment. I have friends in Ohio, who want me to come and work for them. I'm thinking about it. New York is so big, and busy. Write to me at the enclosed address.

Your friend,

Nicolas

Maheeba put the letter in her pocket. "Rose, you must help me write to him. Now, please. I want him to know that I work with you making cones for ice cream. Tell him my name is Mabel and they call me May. He is so handsome."

"He is married," Rose said. "Does he have children?"

"No, he would have said, I know he loves children."

"I'll write your letter," Rose said, getting a pen and paper. "What do you want to say?"

Dear Nicolas,

I got your letter and was happy to hear from you. I pray for your wife.

I am not married and I work for an ice-cream cone factory. It is hard work but I like to work with my friend Rose. She is helping me write this letter. Some day I will write myself. Farouk is fine. We call him Frank. He works for my brothers, Tom and Hashar in the bar. They sell sandwiches too. Maybe some day you will come to Ohio.

Your friend,

Mabel, they call me May

For weeks, Maheeba would get headaches at work. Her only real joy was Nicolas's letters. Rose wrote and read the letters and taught Maheeba to write her name and to write Dear Nicolas. But then Nicolas's letters stopped coming. For months, she did not hear from him, and her condition began to worsen. The intense steam at the cone factory bothered her eyes, and one day after work her friend helped her home.

"Are you alright?" Rose said. "Should I get a doctor?"

"No," Maheeba said. "What do you think happened to Nicolas?"

"I think his wife came to America and you are an imposition," Rose said. "How can he explain you?"

"Do you think he went back to Lebanon?"

"You better forget him and start thinking about your health. Are you alright?"

"I feel sick in my stomach. No doctor, all they do is operate." Maheeba found a chair to sit on. "Please, get my sister-in-law. Look next door. She is a good healer."

When Confidad arrived she found Maheeba lying down in bed.

"What hurts?"

"My head. My stomach is upset and everything looks blurred."

"How long have you felt this way?" Confidad asked, feeling Maheeba's head. She then placed a quarter on her head. Her headache remedy was a cold coin pressed into the forehead.

"A couple of weeks. The blurry vision came on a few days ago. After I lay down it seems to get better. The coin feels good."

"A fifty cent piece would feel better." Confidad sat down on the bed and rubbed Maheeba's forehead. Like a promenade, both of her hands met at the bridge of the nose. Her fingers danced slowly up the forehead, separating and ending just above each ear. Then the three middle fingers worked in a soft circular motion. It was so soothing that Maheeba fell asleep. Quietly the two women left the room.

"What is it?" Rose asked.

"I think she has something wrong with her eyes. The only thing I know is to burn her arm with a hot iron. That draws the poison out. Even doctors do it."

Rose made the sign of the cross. "No, for God's sake."

When Maheeba woke up, they told her. This was standard practice in Syria, and she accepted her fate.

Her brothers and Rose stood around her bed to help.

Confidad handed Maheeba a cup of strong liquor. "Drink this *arak*. I mixed it with honey, a little lemon and water."

As Maheeba drank, it felt like a ball of fire going down her throat, exploding in her stomach and warming her entire body. After the second drink, Maheeba was relaxed, the room was spinning, and she could not focus her eyes.

"Bite down on this," Confidad said, folding a wash cloth. She put another wet cloth across Maheeba's eyes.

Maheeba prayed. Hashar took a skewer, and wrapped the handle with a towel. He immersed the end in a flame until it was red hot, while Tom held his sister's feet and Frank held her right arm. Confidad wiped a spot on the left arm with alcohol and Hashar branded his sister. Maheeba's body convulsed for a few seconds, and then she passed out, immersed in the smell of burning flesh.

After an eternity, she began to surface then slip back, fading in and out of consciousness like a drowning child. The smells and sounds began to penetrate her senses. There were inaudible whispers and unrecognizable scents. Without lifting from the pillow, she turned her head toward the source of discomfort. Her eyes opened slowly and gradually focused on her arm. The pain registered in her brain. She stared at the wet grape leaves that decorated her arm. It felt cold. Her eyes locked onto the foreign mass. "What?" she muttered.

"It's all over, you'll be fine now," Confidad said as she unmasked the herbs. "This will draw the puss out. It's parsley, sage, and garbanzo bean paste. The mint is to make it smell good, the grape leaves keep it moist." She then wrapped a bandage over the healing concoction.

Maheeba eventually recovered, but the scar looked like her skin had been sucked from the inside of her body. Her eyes improved, but she never went back to work at the factory. She did odd jobs, sewing and cleaning houses. Every day she looked at the scar. "It's so ugly," she said, as she covered it up with a long sleeve.

After several months another letter arrived. "It's from Nicolas, I know it," Maheeba thought. She ran to Rose's house. Panting, she handed the letter to her friend. "Read it please, it's from Nicolas." '

Rose took the letter:

My dear friend,

So much has happened. My life has changed. My beautiful wife died of tuberculosis. I went to Lebanon to be with her. There was nothing I could do. We had a few happy days, out in the sunshine. She loved the garden. Then she suffered terribly.

I wish I could see you, my friend, now I need you. My new address is enclosed. I am now living in Canton, about 40 miles from you. May I see you? Would your brothers mind?

I will plan to be in Portsmouth in three weeks, unless you write and tell me not to. I will call on you then. Are you married? It doesn't matter, my intentions are honorable.

Your friend,

Nicolas.

It was a long three weeks. Maheeba counted the days. Finally, on a Sunday afternoon, Maheeba arrived home from church. She walked up the few steps to the porch and noticed the pale green paint was chipping. Then her eyes caught the movement of the porch swing. "Nicolas, it's you. It's really you."

He walked over to her. "The years have been good to you. You are more beautiful than I remembered."

"You look good yourself. Let's sit down and talk. How have you been?"

"Alright, I guess," Nicolas said. "I'm a salesman for a dry goods company. Most of our customers are Arab merchants, so I do fairly well."

Just then her family began to arrive, and Maheeba introduced them. "This is my brother Hashar, his wife and son. You remember my brothers Farouk, its Frank now and Tom. This is my friend Nicolas Thomas."

"Come in," invited Hashar, "*Ahlan wa sahlan.*"

"Frank, do you think we can go to a picture show later?" Nicolas asked, looking at Hashar, who nodded yes.

Frank smiled, "Maybe it will be a cowboy movie."

Maheeba knew that the visit would be pleasant. It was not polite to ask a visitor his business or where he comes from. The women served the men, first *maza,* cheese, tomatoes, hard boiled eggs, and drinks. They ate and drank, while the women prepared dinner.

Nicolas was delighted with the Arabic feast. There was *koosa,* stuffed squash, *batinjan,* baked eggplant, and *kibby.* Maheeba offered him some bread and he took it, tore off a piece and handed the remainder to Tom. "Would you like some Lebanese bread?"

From Tom's glare, Nicolas knew he'd made a mistake.

"Sorry, I meant Arabic bread."

"Syrian bread," Tom said as he tore off a piece and handed it to Hashar. At the end of the meal, Maheeba brought out *backlava* and Turkish coffee to be enjoyed with cigars.

"Let me show you around. We have a garden in the back and fruit trees," Maheeba said as she took Nicolas' hand.

Once they were alone, they never stopped talking.

"I want to see you again," Nicolas said. "I will ask permission."

"Not yet. Let them get used to you first."

"Alright, I will arrange a business trip. We have lots of customers in this area. I will stay for a few weeks."

"It's time to go to the show," Frank yelled from the porch.

Maheeba and Nicolas walked reluctantly to the house.

"Thank you for everything. You have a beautiful family. I will get them back after the show and ice cream." Nicolas said politely.

For weeks, Maheeba and Nicolas saw each other in secret. Maheeba would pretend to work late or go to Rose's house. Nicolas would pick her up and they would drive out of town. They would hold hands and take long walks along the river. Sometimes they would go to the movies. They always hid in the shadows, never to be seen by others.

"It is time I talk to your brothers," Nicolas said. "I want to take you out properly."

"I will meet you right after work and we will go together," Maheeba said. "Hashar is the oldest and maybe he will understand."

He kissed her long and hard. "I'll see you tomorrow."

The next night the two lovers met, and Nicolas drove to the house. He knocked on the door. "Come in, said Confidad, Hashar expects you." She led Nicolas to the sitting room and offered coffee. Maheeba was not permitted to stay.

The women listened from the kitchen. The voices were soft, then louder and angry. "Why?" Nicolas asked. "Because I'm Lebanese or because I am twenty five years old? Doesn't Maheeba have anything to say? This is America. No pre-arranged marriages!"

"Hashar must have said no," Maheeba whispered to Confidad.

"What did you think he would say? You are not fifteen yet. Worse, he's Lebanese."

"I don't care. I love him. He's the best thing that ever happened to me."

The conversation was over. Nicolas got up to leave. "I hope I can see you again," he said to Maheeba. She just looked at him with tears in her eyes.

17

Rendezvous, 1909

Maheeba and Nicolas met often at their secret place, a patch of earth under the stone bridge. There they could sit on the grass, throw rocks into the river, and be safe from their disapproving families. Maheeba sensed the changing season. She loved the huge buckeye tree that hid the entrance and decorated their hideaway with big blue and white clusters of blossoms that looked like little Christmas trees.

"I hate to see summer end. It's like everything is over. Even our tree is shedding and the flowers dying. Oh Nicolas, I don't want it to end."

"I love you Maheeba. I will marry you."

"I love you too, but it won't work. My brothers will never approve. They plan to send me away. Nicolas, this is goodbye. "

"Why, because I am Lebanese? That's crazy. We talk the same language, eat the same food, and worship the same God. We're just the same, Arabs. Besides I'm an American."

"It's the same with your family. They won't accept me because I'm Syrian, and no one will listen. We have no one to turn to."

"I won't give up. I love you." Nicolas kissed her passionately, as though it was the last time. He slowly ran his hands down her blue cotton blouse, noticing the little white daises. He unbuttoned a sleeve, rolled it up and began to kiss her arm. She put her other hand on his. He looked up at her curiously.

"I have a scar, it's ugly."

He carefully resumed rolling up her sleeve. "Oh, he said sympathetically, how did it happen?"

"When I worked at the cone factory, the steam hurt my eyes and I was getting terrible headaches. Confidad and Hashar treated my ailment by burning my arm. I don't have headaches any more and my eyes are better, but I never went back to work."

"You never told me. I'm so sorry." He continued kissing her all the way to her lips. He kissed her hair and inhaled the beautiful aroma of lilacs. "I smell your perfume." Embracing, they slid down to the grass. He wanted her desperately but could only lay there with her and listen to the people on the bridge, leaning on the railing, talking. A few cars went by. The ducks came out of the water and started nesting.

"I'll think of something. Where will they send you? When?" Flashing questions, he tried to stabilize his passion.

"I leave the day after tomorrow, to visit friends in Pittsburgh,. I'll take the train at noon. I love you." Maheeba looked into his face, wanting to remember every little detail. His dark brown eyes, and little mustache, that matched his black curly hair. He was handsome, with his deep tan face and dimpled chin. She wanted to feel his hairy chest but didn't dare invite trouble. He was perfect in every way, slim and muscular, about five inches taller then her five feet two. She looked up at him. The moonlight made her tears sparkle.

He cradled her chin in the palm of his hand, dried each eye with his handkerchief and kissed the lids. "I have a plan. Listen carefully. The train stops at Steubenville. You get off and I will be waiting there at the station. We will get married. You will have your wardrobe with you, it's perfect. They will have to accept us then."

"I am only fifteen. Won't we have to lie about my age?"

"Just a white lie. Put your hair up, like this." He curled her dark brown braid on top of her head. "We'll say you are eighteen."

"It's exciting but I'm scared."

"It's got to work," Nicolas smiled. "Allah is always on the side of lovers."

They kissed and he held her tight. "Can I see you tomorrow?" Nicolas asked.

"I don't know. They're watching me. I said I was going to Rose's house tonight. Hashar didn't want me to go but Confidad talked him into it."

"Good for Confidad," Nicolas said. "I'll send her flowers when we get back."

"Do you know Karl's Auto Shop, on Main Street?" Nicolas asked.

"Yes, the one next to the Drug Store," Maheeba said.

"I'll meet you there tomorrow at eleven o'clock. We will make our plans."

"I can be there," Maheeba said. "My brothers won't be home then. I'll plan to do some shopping."

They kissed good night. He looked at her beautifully shaped body, delicate and graceful, with flawless light olive skin and big dark eyes. "I can't wait until we are married and you are mine."

He waited until she was out of sight, and then he left.

The next day, Nicolas met Maheeba at the garage where his best friend worked. "Sit here," he said dusting off a stool, "while I talk to Karl."

Karl was a short, blond, blue eyed, husky young man of German decent. He was so unlike Nicolas. Even his taste for food, dress, and personality were different. The attraction must have been that they were opposite, like polarized batteries.

"Karl, I need to talk to you. When do you have a break?"

"Not till lunch. I have to get this engine back together. Why?"

Nicolas walked over to his friend but remained far enough away so he wouldn't get dirty. "I have a big favor to ask. That's Maheeba over there, and we are going to run away and get married."

"Just like that?" Karl asked, with out looking up. "Like her brothers won't take out a contract on you!"

"I'm serious," Nicolas said. "They're sending her to Pittsburgh and I'll get her off the train in Steubenville and then we'll get married."

"She's fifteen and you're twenty five. There's a law against that. You're crazy, Nick."

"Aren't you my friend? I would do this for you. Where is your sense of adventure?" Karl slammed the hood down, wiped his greasy hands on his shirt, and faced Nicolas. "Kidnapping a minor from a train. No thanks, I don't need that kind of adventure."

"What kind of a friend are you? I need you to drive. We can take my Ford. Steubenville is only twenty five miles away. I'm going to do it. Once we're married they will have to accept it."

"They could have it annulled."

"Never," Nicolas said. "She'll be a married woman. At least say you will think about it. Come on, I want you to meet her."

They walked over to Maheeba, and she blushed. "Maheeba, this is Karl. He used to be my best friend."

"I'm happy to meet you and I can see why Nick is in love," Karl said. "You're about the prettiest thing I've ever seen. Lunch, twelve o'clock, I'll think about it, but I'm not promising anything."

"Thanks, old friend," Nicolas said slapping Karl's shoulder. "I'll see you at noon. I'll buy lunch." Nicolas took Maheeba by the hand and they walked out.

The next day, Hashar and Confidad took Maheeba to the train station.

Maheeba was nervously thinking about her plans. "I wonder what my family will say when they find out about Nicolas and me running away and getting married. Tom will be mad. Maybe when they see how happy I am, they will understand. I wish I could have brought my wedding dress, but Confidad helped me pack. I wanted to tell her my secret, but she would have to tell Hashar."

The car pulled into the station, and stopped. "We're here," Confidad said. "Have a good trip. Allah be with you."

Maheeba hugged her sister-in-law. "I'm wearing Ime's relic. It will bring me good luck," she said as she boarded the train.

Hashar carried Maheeba's bags and put them in the overhead compartment. "This is the right thing to do," he said. "You will forget Nicolas and we will find you a good Syrian man."

Maheeba nodded her head yes, and said goodbye. She dusted off the maroon velvet seat, settled in by the window and waved goodbye to her family. She saw Karl in the background, waving. "He must be driving with Nicolas," she thought, as the adrenalin surged through her body and her heart began to beat faster. "Please Allah help me. Make this right."

Maheeba was dressed in a white ruffled blouse, a light blue suit with a long skirt, and tight fitted jacket. She carried a matching stole with fringes on the ends and wore her very first hat with blue and white feathers that fanned out in front. Maheeba was light olive skinned, blemish free with no make up.

She set the lunch basket down, took the stole, folded it and laid it on the seat next to her. "This could be my wedding veil," she thought. "I wish I were wearing a white satin wedding dress like the one I'm making." She felt ecstasy thinking of Nicolas, the life they would have. Then she felt agony, the pain of disobeying her brothers, and fear of what her family would say or do. "I wonder if Nicolas will meet the train," she prayed, "and if the conductor will let me leave. Hashar did tell him to take me all the way to Pittsburg!"

Maheeba looked across the aisle at a portly, middle aged man in a gray suit, smoking a cigar. The smell was familiar and pleasant. Like Nicolas's cigars. From the window she could see the highway with only twenty five feet of bare land between them. Across the highway were houses. She watched the ground speed by and listened, mesmerized by the wheels rolling on the tracks. She closed her eyes, trying to relax.

Suddenly, Maheeba was startled by a commotion, something was happening outside the train.

"Look Mommy," a little girl with pig tails shouted, "out the window a man is standing on a car!"

"Maheeba! Maheeba!" Nicolas called, standing on the running board and waving his blue hat. "I love you."

"Get in here." Karl yelled at Nicolas. "Get in here now!"

Nicolas jumped back into the car and leaned his body halfway out of the window. "Maheeba!" He shouted and waved his hat again. The car raced beside the train.

The passengers strained their ears to decipher what the crazy man was yelling. Some of them opened their windows.

"Maheeba! Maheeba, I love you!"

"What is going on?" The porter asked, looking very official in a white shirt and black vest, with a watch and chain hanging from his pocket.

"It's some guy waving at us and calling a woman's name," one of the passengers replied.

Maheeba opened her window and shouted, "Nicolas, Nicolas it's you!" She waved, and her long shawl blew in the wind. She could see Karl driving the black Ford sedan. He wore brown overalls and a plaid shirt. Their contrast in dress was obvious. Nicolas wore a navy blue pin striped suit, with a white shirt and matching tie.

"Do you know this fellow?" the porter asked sternly.

Maheeba tried to contain the child within her, who wanted to jump up and down and clap her hands. "Yes, we're going to be married, but my brothers don't approve. They're sending me away."

A woman in a yellow dress and hat carrying a barking poodle butted in. "Why, what's wrong with him?"

"He's—he's an American and they want me to marry a Syrian."

"Do you love him?"

"Yes, he's the most wonderful man in the world!"

"Steubenville," Nicolas shouted. "I'll meet you there!"

The train made a short stop and the car went on ahead.

A short, fat, soft-spoken man with a beard, looking concerned, leaned over the aisle. "What do you plan to do?"

"He's going to meet me at the next station, if I can get off the train. Then we'll get married."

Across the aisle, a gray haired, elderly lady in a pink bonnet with a matching plaid dress, stood up. Bracing herself against the seat in front, she shouted, "We Americans ought to stick together and help this young lady! How many are getting off at the next stop, besides me?"

Several people raised their hands.

"We'll just put you in the middle and walk off this train together. Just let some one try to stop us," she said shaking her pink umbrella. "What is your name, my dear?"

"Maheeba. It's Mabel in English, or May."

"Mabel, your friends in Pittsburgh, won't they be worried?"

"Yes, I think so, they're very nice."

"Why don't you send them a telegram and let them know you've changed your plans."

"How can I do that?"

"There's a telegraph office at the train depot. You can send one from there."

The train began to slow down as the brakes grounded to a halt.

"Steubenville!" The conductor announced.

"Come on, Deary. We will walk you to the station."

"Here let me carry that for you," offered a tall well-dressed gentleman with a cane.

Maheeba stepped down. Nicolas was still waving his hat. She ran into his arms, and he lifted her up and twirled her around. She had to hold on to her hat, as they kissed and embraced tightly. Everyone cheered and applauded, even those who didn't know what the happy occasion was about. Passengers on the train yelled and waved. "Good luck! God bless you!"

"See," Nicolas said, "Allah is on the side of lovers! You remember Karl?"

"We met at the garage. I never forget a beautiful face," Karl said, bowing. "Do I get to kiss the bride?"

"No," Nicolas said, standing in front of Maheeba and pushing her behind him, "not before the wedding, and you'll be damned lucky then."

The gray haired lady walked up to the couple. "I'm Mrs. Kent, and I live here. Would you like to come to my house for some tea and freshen up?"

"Thank you," Nicolas said shaking her hand. "You have done so much already, but we have to drive onto Canton, where I have friends. We're going to get married."

They said their goodbyes and waved at the passengers on the train.

"Nicolas," Maheeba said. "Can we send a telegram to my friends in Pittsburgh, so they won't worry?"

"Sure, give me the name and address."

They went to the station where a little old man was sitting at a desk, writing. A halo of gray hair crowned his bald head. He looked up, adjusted his glasses and tipped his visor.

"We want to send a telegram." Nicolas said, handing him the address.

The operator picked up his pencil and pulled up his black arm band, "What do you want to say?"

"I got off the train in Steubenville," Maheeba said. "I'm going to get married. Please tell my brothers not to worry. Thank you. Maheeba."

"Okay, that will be fifty cents."

Nicolas paid the man. They picked up their bags and headed for the car.

"Will you go with us and be my best man?" Nicolas asked Karl.

"I was counting on it," Karl said as he pulled out the keys and slid into the driver's seat. "I even brought a sports jacket." They put the suitcases in the trunk and the lovers climbed into the back seat.

Nicolas put his arms around Maheeba and kissed her head. "I promise you a beautiful life. There will never be a conflict in our home. I will even learn to call it Syrian bread. I love you." Looking up he said, "Karl, when do you have to return to work?"

"I took a week for vacation, in case you want me to go along on the honey-moon."

"No thanks, I think I can handle it all by myself."

"Nick, how are you going to pull this off? "What are your plans?"

"I have friends in Canton, Maheeba will stay with them and we can stay in my apartment. I won't disappoint her. We will have a church wedding, white dress and all." Nicolas looked down and saw a smile on Maheeba's face.

Looking in the rear view mirror, Karl asked, "What should I give as a wedding present?"

"In Syria, you would give a goat or a lamb, but your being here is the best gift."

"You have a beautiful woman," Karl said. "Maybe I should go to Syria and find an Arab bride."

"Not a chance. The fathers would hide their daughters," Nicolas said. "Wake me when we get to Canton."

Karl turned on the radio and listened quietly.

Maheeba leaned back, and closed her eyes to dream of her new life,.

18

Canton, Ohio, 1909

It was early evening when they arrived in Canton. They drove to Nicolas' friend's house. It was a modest home in a middle class neighborhood. It had a white picket fence, enclosing a lovely yard. The grass was well trimmed and multi-colored geraniums bordered the front porch. Nicolas opened the gate, led the way, and rang the doorbell.

"Welcome to our home," said the lady of the house. She was slender, in her mid-twenties, with dark eyes and olive skin. Her hair was mussed and she wore an apron over her plain pink housedress. "Thank God you arrived safely. This must be Maheeba. She is beautiful, come in, make yourself at home."

"This is my bride to be and my friend Karl," Nicolas said. "Maheeba, Karl, meet Mary and Bill Lewis, my partner." They all shook hands, and were escorted into the living room for food and drinks.

"Are you very hungry?" Mary asked. "Dinner is almost ready."

"We're fine," Nicolas said. "We ate the lunch that Maheeba had packed."

"I'll leave you men to talk," Mary said.

Maheeba got up and offered to help with dinner. In the kitchen, Mary asked about the wedding. "Will you be married here? We have St. Mary's, a beautiful Orthodox Church."

"I want to be married in Portsmouth, at St. Anthony's Church with all my family there. It's what I dreamed of."

"I understand," Mary said. "Do you have a wedding gown? I have my white dress and veil, if you would like to borrow it."

"I brought my beautiful satin robe from Syria," Maheeba said. "But it is not finished."

The conversation was interrupted with the sound of a baby crying. "It never fails; he knows when dinner is ready."

Maheeba followed Mary to the baby's room. "This is Edward, he is nine months old." Mary changed his diaper, picked him up and patted his back. The baby turned around to look at the stranger.

"Can I hold him?" Maheeba asked as she held out her arms. The baby willingly leaned toward her and she kissed him on the cheek. The two bonded immediately.

"What a beautiful boy."

They returned to the kitchen. "Would you like to feed him?" Mary asked as she offered Maheeba the bottle.

Maheeba accepted and sat down. After he finished his bottle the baby fell asleep in her arms. "I'll put him back in bed." Maheeba looked at the baby lying in the crib. "I hope I have a boy like you." She turned out the light and returned to the kitchen.

"What can I do?" Maheeba asked.

"The table is all set. Why don't you mix the salad," Mary said, as she took a lamb roast out of the oven. "This is Nicolas' favorite."

"It's beautiful, and smells so good," Maheeba said.

"We have green beans and rice to go with it. Tell Bill we're ready."

The women served, and then sat down. During dinner they talked about the wedding.

"Karl and I will go back to Portsmouth and I will talk to Hashar," Nicolas said. "If he won't be reasonable, we will get married in Canton. Can she stay here for a few days?"

"As long as you like," Bill said, looking at Maheeba.

"I'll show you my veil," Mary said excitedly. "It has a crown of white lace and lilies of the valley. If you like it, I will gift it to you. We will have such fun planning. I will be your big sister."

After dinner they visited for a while, and then Karl and Nicolas said goodnight and left.

In the morning, they all had breakfast together, and then Karl and Nicolas drove back to Portsmouth.

Later that day, Mary and Maheeba were visiting while doing household chores. They were in the kitchen making dinner when the phone rang. Mary picked up the receiver. "Nick. Where are you?"

"I'm calling from Karl's garage. It's good news. Let me talk to Maheeba."

"Hello? Nicolas!"

"Darling, we can be married in Portsmouth!"

Maheeba dropped the receiver and turned to Mary, jumping up and down, "He did it! He did it! I can go home to be married!"

"Maheeba, Maheeba," Nicolas' voice could be heard. "Pick up the phone."

Mary picked it up. "I heard. She's on cloud nine."

"Well," Nicolas said, "the bad news is we have to wait six months. I promised her brothers."

"Why?"

"She will be sixteen then. But I think the real reason is to try and persuade her not to marry me."

"Don't worry, that will never happen," Mary said. "When will you get here?"

"Tomorrow. I have a lot of things to do. Tell Bill I'm moving to Portsmouth."

"Let me talk to him," begged Maheeba. "I can't believe it," she said, taking the phone. "Tell me everything. Was Hashar mad? What did Tom say?"

"I told them that we are in love and I promised to take good care of you," Nicolas said. "I asked if we could be married in Portsmouth with their blessing. Hashar said I didn't give him much choice, but you are always welcome in his home. He loves you, and offered a dowry."

"How much?" Maheeba interrupted.

"Three hundred dollars," Nicolas said. "I told him we didn't need it, but he insisted. Tom is still mad and wouldn't shake hands. I have to go now. I won't see you until tomorrow, about noon. I love you, my darling. Good-bye for now."

"I love you too." Maheeba hung up the phone and turned to Mary. "Tomorrow! I have to get ready. My dress, it's not finished yet."

"Calm down, you have six months to get ready. Your brothers requested that you wait that long and Hashar will give you away."

"In six months I'll be sixteen." She thought about it, and then said, "It will go fast. I'll make it go fast. I want to change my wedding dress. It's a robe like the old country. I want an American gown, like the magazine."

"You can take it to a seamstress and have the old and new all in one. It will be beautiful."

"Old and new," Maheeba said. "I like the sound of that very much."

Nicolas worked hard over the next six months, and Maheeba marveled at his ingenuity. He sold his share of the store to Bill, and then he contracted with the dry goods manufacturer to manage the Tri-State area, including Southern Pennsylvania, West Virginia and Ohio. He received a commission, plus a bonus for each new client, and then hired salesmen to work for him. It was not long before he prospered. Before the six months were up, he bought a small house, and a year later he purchased a three-story apartment building with a Pool Room on the street level. Within ten years, he would amass a fortune, including several houses, an ice-cream parlor and stock in the coal mines.

Maheeba's brothers tried to dissuade her from marrying Nicolas with a parade of Syrian bachelors. Some were tall, some short, some slim, some fat, and from ages twenty to forty. The agenda was always the same. After dinner, Maheeba was left with her suitor to give him the opportunity to persuade her, and discuss his virtues. Tom tried to make a case for Joseph Lahood, to no avail. "Why don't you be smart? He's a good Syrian. You marry him." That episode, as well as most of the others, led to tears. Her sister-in-law usually sided with her, and Hashar always insisted that Maheeba could decide.

"I'm going to Syria to find a bride," Tom told Maheeba. "I am thirty years old, it is time I marry. I wish you would go with me, and find a nice Syrian man."

"I will stay here with Nicolas," Maheeba said. "I hope you find a good wife and be happy like me."

As agreed upon, Maheeba was allowed to date Nicolas whenever he was in town. When the six months passed, Nicolas and Maheeba were still madly in love. On April 26, 1910, Maheeba and Nicolas Thomas were married at St. Anthony's Church in Portsmouth, Ohio. The bride wore a beautiful white, high colored lace dress over satin. A wide satin band cinched her tiny waist. The gown had hand-embroidered flowers on the skirt. The long veil, a gift from Mary, was attached to a crown of lace and lilies-of-the-valley. The groom wore matching flowers in his lapel. Karl Schmitt was best man and Rose Bryan was maid of honor. Hashar gave her away and Frank was ring bearer. Tom was in Syria, and did not attend. The couple planned to honeymoon in New York. No one mentioned that some members of the family refused to attend because Nicolas was Lebanese.

Following the ceremony, Nicolas presented his bride with a gold cameo necklace as a gift in honor of the event. The guests and the bridal party celebrated with a feast of American and Syrian foods at the church hall. Festivities lasted all day, with singing and dancing. The ladies loved to get Karl to dance. The belly dancer threw her silk scarf around Karl's neck and pulled him to the dance floor. He tried to follow the fast moving steps and the hip movement.

"Get me out of this!" He shouted to Maheeba, who pulled Nicolas out of his seat and pushed him to the dancer. Nicolas held up his hands, snapped his fingers and did the fancy footwork.

As Karl sat down, the fat woman next to him whispered, "You say *hissy hissy teasie*, make her go fast." Karl shouted what he thought was "dance faster"!

Frank walked over to Karl and said, "You're telling her to shake her ass." Karl looked at the woman and shook his head. She laughed.

Nicolas pulled out his handkerchief and twirled it in the air. He reached for Maheeba's hand and pulled her beside him. She grabbed Karl's hand. The other guests joined in to form a line and dance the *dubkee.*

At the end of the wedding feast, guests were given a white mesh bag with three Jordan almonds. The candy-coated nuts signified a sweet and prosperous life. Before leaving, each guest said to the bride, "*Nikshalak arees,* May you be blessed with a boy".

Nicolas took Maheeba to his house, which they had furnished modestly. There was a lot more to be done, but it was theirs. Before Maheeba entered her new home, she noticed a section of *ahjeen,* dough, which her sister-in-law had pasted on the doorsill above the entrance. She walked under it, and the dough stuck, signifying a long and happy life for the couple. Nicolas picked her up in his arms and carried her up the stairs to the bedroom. Maheeba giggled as she threw her arms around his neck. "What are you doing?"

"It's an American custom, to carry your bride across the threshold." He laid her down on the bed, kissed her and rolled her over on top of him. They looked into each other's eyes. She was scared and he was nervous.

While Maheeba was in the bathroom getting ready, Nicolas undressed and climbed into bed. When she returned and stood at the foot of the bed, he stared at this vision of loveliness, now his own. Her beauty and grace were sensuous to Nicolas. Her long, black hair caressed her shoulders. Her flawless skin and big brown eyes glowed. Her small frame hidden under the white silk gown, revealed her shapely body. She was the most beautiful creature he had ever seen. He pulled back the covers and she slid into bed beside him. He slowly slid his hands under her gown feeling every inch of her body. She was nervous.

"It will be a good life," he promised, and she smiled, "Yes."

19

A good life, 1910

A month had gone by, and Maheeba was happy. Nicolas fixed up the house and had it painted. Keeping house and canning vegetables was so much easier than in Syria. "Ime," she said. "It's a good life. Nicolas is a kind man, and smart. He works very hard, and never gets mad. I like to wash his feet, like Papa. I hope you can see me."

One day Maheeba was busily working around the house, when the doorbell rang. She wiped her hands on her apron and answered the door. "Karl, what are you doing here? Nicolas wont be home for another hour."

"I came to see the lady of the house, with a wedding present. Don't I get a hug?"

Although she was uncomfortable making physical contact with men, she held out her hand to shake. Karl looked at her open hand, "That won't do." He threw his arms around her, "An American bear hug." He grinned his infectious grin as Maheeba blushed. "Do I get invited in for a cup of that Turkish coffee?"

"Well, yes, let me go next door for a minute. You can sit on the swing. I'll be right back."

"Hey," Karl said, "I almost forgot your wedding gift."

Maheeba followed him to the porch railing where he untied a rope.

"A goat!" she said laughing. "In the name of the Father, what'll I do with it?"

"I don't know," Karl said, patting the shaggy white animal on the back. "What do Syrians do? Make *joban*, goat cheese. Nanny Goat meet Maheeba. She's your new owner."

"She is cute, and healthy," Maheeba said, looking into the goat's face. "Like we had in the old country."

"I'll put her in the garage till Nick gets home," Karl said, as he led his prize down the driveway, into the one car garage and closed the door.

When he was out of sight, Maheeba ran to her neighbor's house and knocked. Susan came to the door, drying her hands on a towel. She pushed her blond hair out of her face and smiled. She was tall and very attractive, in her late forties.

"Please, can you come over and visit, have a cup of coffee? Nicolas' friend is there and wants to wait till my husband gets home."

"And you never entertained a man alone," Susan said.

Maheeba shook her head. "American men are bold. I don't know what the neighbors would say. What Nicolas would think?"

"Okay, I'll be right with you. I made some blackberry jam, and I'll give you a jar to go with the coffee. You can say you came to borrow some."

"Oh, thank you so much."

When the women returned, Karl was sitting on the porch swing. "This is Karl Schmitt," Maheeba said, "and this is my good friend and neighbor, Susan. She made some jam for us. Come in and I will put the coffee on. Karl, tell her about the gift."

"It wasn't easy to get a live goat," Karl said laughing. "I had to order it from the butcher, it took a month. Nick said it was a Syrian custom. Did you really have goats?"

"Is he joking?" Susan asked. "What on earth will you do with it?"

"I milked lots of goats, but we didn't have to keep them in a garage," Maheeba said, setting out the coffee. She brought out some Syrian bread with cheese, olives, fruit and jam. Maheeba heated the cream and poured it simultaneously with the coffee, into demitasse cups and added honey.

"Is the coffee too strong for you, Susan?"

"No, it is very good."

"This jam is delicious. My favorite," Karl raved.

"I'll get you a jar to take home," Susan said, getting up to leave.

"No, let him take mine and I'll get more later," Maheeba insisted, holding on to Susan's arm.

"Good idea."

"If you hated the Turks, why do you drink their coffee?" Karl asked Maheeba.

"They brought it to Syria. The Arabs liked that strong stuff. It gives you a jolt."

"Susan, do you know the best part of Turkish coffee is telling fortunes after. Will you, please?" Karl asked Maheeba, as he inverted his cup into the saucer.

Maheeba picked up the cup. "You will have a long and prosperous life, with a beautiful, patient wife, and many children." She turned the cup in her hand. "I see goats, many goats in the near future. They are flooding your apartment, on your furniture, everywhere. Oh my, the noise, the smell, they are destroying your place."

"That's enough," Karl laughed. "I get the picture."

"Oh look," Maheeba said, "Nicolas is home."

Nicolas got out of the car and came into the house He kissed his wife on the forehead. "When did you get here?" he asked as he shook Karl's hand.

"Not soon enough. I didn't have much time with the ladies."

"I better go home now," Susan said. "It was nice meeting you, Karl, enjoy the jam. I'll bring you some tomorrow, Mabel."

"Thank you for coming," Maheeba said walking her to the door.

"Mabel?" Karl looked puzzled.

"My American name. They even call me May," Maheeba said.

She returned to the kitchen and poured Nicolas some coffee. Maheeba then fetched a pan of warm water and set it down at his feet. "Not now," Nicolas said waving her away.

"What is this?" Karl asked. "You bathe his feet, like in the Bible?"

"Doesn't every woman?" Maheeba snapped.

"No, I'm jealous. I want a Syrian wife. If he ever gives you a hard time," Karl said reaching for Maheeba's hand.

"Show Nicolas what you brought us," Maheeba said, pulling away from Karl.

"You brought a gift?"

"What every house should have. A goat, in the garage."

The trio walked down the driveway. As they approached the garage, they could hear the sound of something ramming against wood. The goat had chewed a hole in the door and was trying to enlarge it by butting his way to freedom.

"Damn, it's destroying the garage," Nicolas said. "When I open the door you try to grab her rope"

Nicolas raised the garage door, and the goat squeezed through the first visible opening. It easily knocked Karl down and ran.

"Whoa, stop, come back, here girl. Heel!" Karl yelled, running across the neighbor's yard.

"I wish I had a camera," Nicolas said.

Sensing her pursuer had hesitated, the goat stopped to eat the irresistible green vegetation in the garden. Karl walked up slowly, grabbed the leash, and led her back to her new owners.

"What will you do for an encore?" Nicolas asked.

"I don't know but you cannot refuse a gift, so Nanny is all yours."

"Put Nanny in your truck and we can take her to Albert's farm. Of all the hair brained ideas you've come up with, this takes the cake. You will have to fix the garage door," Nicolas said. "Maheeba, we'll be back in two hours."

She watched the truck pull away and walked into the house. "Ime, I have a goat," Maheeba said. "How many times we milked a goat together and made *joban*. We never get goat cheese here, but I don't care. Life in America is so easy. We have a beautiful three bedroom house with a gas stove and running water. I have a garden in the backyard with tomatoes, mint, parsley, onions, and corn. Did you ever eat corn? I am so happy and Nicolas is kind and loving, not like other Syrian men. You know, I never saw Papa kiss you. Ime, I'm going to have a baby. Allah, give me a boy?"

Another month went by, and Tom returned from Damascus with his young bride, Nadia. She was very pretty, frail and looked much older than her eighteen years. Maheeba gave the couple a warm welcome with a big family party. She greeted Nadia with a hug, "Welcome to our home. How was your trip?" Maheeba asked, as they walked into the kitchen.

"I was sick with child. Two weeks, I can't eat or sleep," Nadia said as she began to cry. "I am afraid of your brother. He has a sharp voice. I'm not used to a man and I don't know how to cook."

"I'm pregnant too," Maheeba said as she hugged her sister-in-law. "My brother is strict, but he is a good man and will take care of you. You don't cook? How can your mother let you marry, and not cook?"

"I went to school, and was a teacher for two years. I lived with my mother and I miss her," Nadia said as she began to cry again.

"I will teach you to cook and you can help me read," Maheeba said. "We will be good friends. Tomorrow you come for coffee and we will talk. Now we will have a good time. You will like America."

The next day Nadia came to visit. She looked more refreshed. "Come in," Maheeba said. "We will cook dinner together. Tell me everything. How did you meet Tom?"

"Your brother walked the streets of Damascus for two weeks looking at all the women," Nadia said. "One day he came to Takia, where I teach school. He told me that he sat on a park bench, waiting for destiny to take his hand. Then he noticed me with my group of young school children in blue and white uniforms leaving school. "That's it," Tomas said. I was the one. He watched me discharge my children to their mothers and return to the class room. He sat there and waited for me to come out, and then he followed me home. Tomas said I was like a snake charmer. He came to my house and knocked on the door. When I opened the door and saw him, I didn't know who he was."

"Your father home?" he asked.

"No, he is dead," I said. "May he rest in Peace?"

"I talk to your mother."

My mother is old and tired. She worked so hard all her life, she never smiled. Tomas said he studied my mother's features, trying to find the similarity between her and me.

"I want to marry your daughter," he said. "I am Thomas, son of Mykhal Bakeer from Hums. I come from America to find a good Syrian woman."

"Just like that, he wanted to marry me. My mother invited him in. She told him we have no money, no dowry. He didn't care. Tomas promised to take good care of me. After a while my mother said yes, if he would bring her to America too. He said he didn't have enough money and he would send for her later. After he left, I sat on the floor and put my head in my mother's lap and cried and cried, all night. I was so scared. My mother cried too. She said we had no money. Women in Syria can't own property. Our house belonged to my uncle and he could throw us out anytime. I cried myself to sleep."

"You didn't know my brother? How long did you wait?"

"One week."

"Did you have a big wedding?" Maheeba asked. "Did you see my brother Charles and Sariya?"

"Yes," Nadia said. "They are very nice. We had a small wedding."

"Now we will have our babies together." Maheeba said. "We will be like sisters."

Eight months later Maheeba and Nicolas had their first child. She woke up in the delivery room. No one she knew went to the hospital for childbirth. "Many times I helped Confidad deliver babies in the home," Maheeba said to Nicolas. "This was so much nicer and you brought me flowers. I am so sorry it's not a boy. Are you disappointed?"

"It's a beautiful girl," Nicolas said, holding her hand. "I want to name her Marie, after my mother. We can have a boy next time."

When relatives saw the baby for the first time, they puffed into the infant's face, after complimenting the parents. This superstition was to dispel the evil eye, which guests may not know they have. The old country beliefs were a part of Maheeba. When the baby got diarrhea, Maheeba did not consider it to be an intestinal disorder, but rather the result of the evil eye. She took Marie to her sister-in-law.

"Confidad, my baby is sick," Maheeba said. "I don't know who did this, maybe someone at the store. What can I do? Everything she eats comes out."

"The spell can only be broken by wrapping an onion in the baby's dirty diaper. We tie it and throw it into the river."

The ladies worked diligently to undo the curse. They walked to the bridge and dropped the bundle into the water; Confidad made the sign of the cross and said a prayer.

Relying on instinct and the help of her sister-in-law, Maheeba became a very good mother. For Marie's two o'clock feeding, Maheeba took her to bed with Nicolas. He leaned on his elbow and watched his wife nurse their baby.

When the baby was six months old, Maheeba said, "It is time for some solid food." She dipped her finger into the homemade apple sauce and offered it to her baby. Marie's little hands wrapped around her mother's finger, as she sucked on the sweet fruit. "You like it? Let's try some mashed potatoes and maybe bread, soaked in milk."

When Maheeba boiled chicken to make soup, she would chew the meat until it was very soft. Like a mother bird feeding its young, she took it out of her mouth, and passed it to her off spring.

Nicolas enjoyed his baby. When Marie was baptized, they had a big celebration that lasted all day. Nicolas held his child, and danced with her in his arms. He took pride in showing her off to his friends.

"Ime, I am so happy, even if it is a girl," Maheeba said. "Maybe the next one will be a boy. It is a good life. I never want to go back to Syria."

The following year they had another beautiful girl, Teresa. "Ime, I have not given him a son. You said I will have lots of boys. When? Nicolas didn't get mad. He said it doesn't matter. We make more babies. But my brothers tell me I need to have a boy." Maheeba worried and felt guilty. "In Syria," she thought, "a man can divorce his wife for not giving him a son. Ime help me."

She loved the girls and sang them to sleep with songs from her homeland. Maheeba dressed them in pretty long dresses and bonnets. Both girls were pretty with brown eyes and dark curly hair.

"Marie is very beautiful," Nicolas said, picking her up. "But she is stubborn," he said, as she struggled to get out of his arms. "Not like Teresa who is always smiling."

Nicolas seemed delighted, and enjoyed showing off his children. "I make beautiful babies," he said to his friends. In the evening when Maheeba brought the girls in to play on the floor by Nicolas, he would put them on his lap. He held one on each knee and dangled his watch in their ear. "Your mother tells you stories about her farm in Syria," he said. "I lived in a big city and some day we will visit there."

20

The first son, 1913

Nadia had two children, a boy and a girl. The women visited daily. While the children played together, the mothers made grape jelly, or canned vegetables. Nadia read a recipe for making cookies, and this became a new treat for the families.

Nicolas enjoyed playing with the girls as he listened to the radio. He often tuned into children stories. He watched his wife put the children to bed and sing them to sleep with folk songs.

"Ime," Maheeba prayed, "I don't want to get pregnant right away. I want boys but not so soon. Teresa isn't one year old yet. She is just learning to walk and talk. She said 'Daddy' today. I am afraid if I have another girl Nicolas will get mad at me. I love him and he loves me. I can't ask him to abstain. I'm fasting so I won't make babies. Is it a sin? I want a little more time with the girls, so Nicolas gets use to them. Then, if it's another girl maybe he wont mind. We go to the lake every weekend and he seems so happy. Please make God understand."

For weeks she fasted, eating very little food, and no meat. When Nicolas noticed that she was not eating, he asked, "Are you sick?"

"No, I'm not hungry," Maheeba said.

"You eat," Nicolas insisted.

Maheeba ate only in Nicolas' presence. It was to no avail. When she became pregnant she stopped fasting. "I'm going to have a baby," Maheeba thought. "I'm afraid, it might be a girl. Ime, I pray for a boy."

Nine months later came a boy, the first of five. They named him Tomas, after Maheeba's brother, and called him Tom Tom. Unlike the girls, he was fair skinned with light, almost blond curly hair. He was weak and sickly.

Although it was his first son, Nicolas never bonded with the child. He rejected him and showed his dislike. Maheeba would try to get Nicolas to hold Tom Tom but he would say, "Not now," and go play with the girls.

Maheeba blamed herself for the baby's illness. "It's my fault," she thought. "God must be angry because I tried not to get pregnant. Nicolas never smiles at our baby. Why doesn't he like Tom Tom? Allah, please forgive me?"

When the baby was Baptized, Karl Schmitt came to the Christening. "You have a beautiful son," he said to Nicolas, patting him on the back. "What's his name?"

"Tomas."

"Tomas, Thomas?" Karl asked.

"We call him Tom Tom."

"You should be very happy."

"He doesn't look like me," Nicolas said. Not Lebanese. He has blond hair."

"You got lucky," Karl laughed.

"I don't think that's funny. Everything is a joke with you," Nicolas said.

"What's eating you?"

"I don't know? I really don't know," Nicolas said. "You're my best friend, and you're Aryan. It can't be that I am prejudiced. I travel a lot and Maheeba's alone—with two babies. She is a beautiful woman, and a good wife. She wouldn't cheat. I must not think such things."

"Look in the mirror, crazy man," Karl said. "Your mustache is red and you have a redheaded nephew. Face it, the Crusaders and those Vikings were all over the Mediterranean. He is a throw back, and a very pretty baby."

"I guess you're right," Nicolas said. I am going to be a better father he promised himself.

"Ime," Maheeba said, "my boy is not right. Nicolas never says anything, and tries to be a good father but I know he doesn't like his son."

Tom Tom was frail and often sick. He acted frightened around his father and even flinched when Nicolas made a sudden move. The child was learning disabled and slower to talk, to walk, slower than the girls and he developed a tremor at an early age. Maheeba was overprotective and continued to feel guilt and remorse for not wanting this child.

"Nicolas is mean to Tom Tom," Maheeba said to Nadia. "The girls do something wrong, he laughs. If Tom Tom does the same thing, he gets mad."

"Tomas is that same way with Pete," Nadia said. James can get away with anything. I don't know why they pick on one."

Nicolas continued to prosper. He had a forceful personality and was brilliant. He bought several houses by mortgaging one to pay cash for another. He was generous with his family, and always showered them with gifts. It was the best of times, the American dream fulfilled.

On their fourth wedding anniversary Nicolas bought a farm in Weirton, about twenty acres of good crops—corn, tomatoes, and some fruit trees. "I will get a cow, some chickens, and goats," Nicolas thought. "Maheeba will be happy. It is only twenty-five miles away, so Nadia can visit. She'll love it."

In a happy mood, Nicolas stopped at a road side produce stand. "How much for watermelons?"

"Thirty five cents."

"They are too ripe. I give you twenty five cents," Nicolas said. "Four for a dollar."

"It's late. I'm closing. Take them."

Pleased with his bartering power, Nicolas lined them up on the back seat. "What a good purchase," he thought. "We have a watermelon eating contest."

Daydreaming, he almost missed a stop sign. Slamming on the brakes suddenly, the car bolted and all four of his prized melons fell on the floor, bursting open and spilling sweet succulent juice all over the car.

When Nicolas arrived home, the three children ran to meet him. "Daddy, daddy, what did you bring?"

Marie ran to the car and grabbed the back door handle. Throwing open the dam gates; she released a river of juice, drowning her shoes. "What...?"

"An accident. Clean it up," Nicolas mumbled as he walked to the house.

Maheeba came with bags and rags. "Allah, what a shame." She picked up the pieces of rind and put them in a bucket. The children ate hands full of the fruit before it landed in the garbage can. There was little to salvage. Maheeba wiped up the floor. "Get a bucket of water. We scrub."

The car smelled like watermelon for weeks and the children never missed the opportunity to comment.

"What happened?" Maheeba asked.

"Don't ask." Nicolas said. "I wanted something special to tell you the good news. I bought a farm."

"Where?"

"Weirton."

"A farm!" Maheeba said. "I'm so happy. Like the old country. We take Nanny. Why did you buy a farm? You don't even like going to cousin Albert's."

"It'll be good for the children," Nicolas said. "It must be a lot of work. I never lived on a farm,"

"It's good strong work, and clean air," Maheeba said. "How soon?"

"I will keep my job in town," Nicolas said. "Maybe I'll cut back and help on the farm. We'll leave in a month. Start packing."

21

Life on the farm, 1915

The family moved to a beautiful working farm with corn, tomatoes and a few other crops already planted. The four bedrooms, one and a half bath, house was fairly modern, with running water and electricity. The large porch was perfect for the swing and a couple of chairs. There was a water pump in the front yard that tapped into the well.

While living in Weirton, Maheeba became pregnant with her fourth child. She frequently dreamt of Syria and her father. It was the same reoccurring dream. She would hear her father calling, "Maheeba, Maheeba, come my daughter."

"Papa, where are you? I can't see you." She could see herself walking, and then running through a grove of olive trees, following the sound of his voice.

She saw him, always in the same place, always smiling. His well-trimmed beard was more red than black. He was standing on the edge of the river, his hands in the air, snapping his fingers and dancing.

The setting sun made the blue water sparkle. It matched his shiny robe and headscarf. Maheeba would look at her own clothes, her nightgown transformed into an ornate deep red gown with gold trim. And she was wearing her 'slave' snake bracelet.

Papa would hold his hand out to his daughter, she would grab it and hold tight. He would twirl his handkerchief with the other hand, and they would side-step—sway and hop to the music of *Syria the Beautiful*. They would sing as they did so many times, around the fire. Then his hand would slip out of hers as he danced into the water.

"Papa don't go, please stay," she pleaded.

He would only smile and dance. The distance between them would grow.

"Papa, I love you. I never told you before, but in America, we can say such things." Her legs collapsed and she sat on the rocky ground. "Please come back. I'm going to have a baby."

"I know," he would say, his silhouette disappearing into the horizon.

"I'll name him Mykhal," she would whisper. Then she would stretch out her hand, trying desperately to reach him. Suddenly the water burst into flames.

Screaming, "Paapaa," she awoke, trembling as if she really could feel the heat of the fire. Her body bolted up, and instinctively, she felt for the baby.

"What's the matter?" Nicolas asked, sitting up and turning on the light.

"I saw Papa again."

"How are things on the other side? Did he have a halo, or the other?"

"Don't joke about such things," she said making the sign of the cross.

"I'm sorry. Was it a good dream?" Nicolas slid back under the covers and turned out the light.

"Yes, it was beautiful. I want to name our son Mykhal, Michael, after my father."

"How do you know it will be a boy? I don't think a daughter would like that name."

"I know," Maheeba said confidently. She fluffed the pillow, and rested her head to relive the dream.

As the months went by, Nicolas seemed very happy. He often brought his wife flowers, and a candy treat for the children. One day Maheeba was cleaning vegetables at the sink, while the children were playing in the yard. Nicolas snuck up behind her, patted Maheeba's stomach, and said, "How is my little girl, named Michael?"

"You can joke, but it will be a boy. You will see," Maheeba said. "He will be strong, and handsome, like you."

Nicolas stood behind his wife, and put his arms around her. "I hope this is my baby," he whispered.

Maheeba was startled. "Was he joking?" she thought. She turned around and looked into his eyes. "It is our baby. Why do you say such a thing?"

"I don't know. A bad joke I guess. I want him to look like the girls, like me. Tom Tom is different."

"I didn't fast. He will be a strong boy, like Papa said."

"Do you see your Papa anymore?" Nicolas asked, as he walked over to the table, and sat down.

"No, never again. I miss him. Do you miss your Papa?"

"I never missed my father," Nicolas said. "He was mean and I hated him."

Maheeba brought him a cup of coffee, and sat down. "We will have many sons, like Ime said. You will be proud."

Nicolas pulled his wife onto his lap, and put his hand on her stomach. "I love you and Michael."

It was a dark haired boy. Nicolas was at her side when she delivered. He held his son in his arms and said, "Hello Michael, welcome to America."

Maheeba smiled. "What a beautiful picture," she thought. "I have it all, just like Ime said, a husband like Papa, sons, and a farm."

She and the children enjoyed living on the farm. The girls would milk the cow and goat, and Maheeba would make cheese. After Confidad died, Hashar would visit often with his two children. Once a week he would bring Nadia and her children to the farm. The women would make jelly, dry mint, and can vegetables. The little girls made corn-stalk dolls, and the boys played a horseshoe game. Hashar would do odd jobs around the house, and get the children to pick vegetables. In the fall they gathered walnuts and set them out to dry.

Nanny, the goat, became the family pet and companion. She would follow Maheeba every where. When she stopped to rest, Nanny would lay her head on her owners lap. "You are like a dog," Maheeba said. "Don't you know you're a goat?"

Nicolas spent more and more time in town. He worked harder and avoided the farm. He showed no interest or pleasure in the animals or the garden.

Karl visited often. "You are early," Maheeba said. "Nicolas is not home yet."

"Good, then I can enjoy your company without him," Karl said. "I brought a wagon for the kids. We can harness Nanny and she could pull it like a cart. How's Nanny?"

"She acts like one of the children," Maheeba said, as she led him into the back yard.

"She plays with them and tries to chew up their ball. Come and see."

"How are you?" Karl asked, as he put his hand on Maheeba's shoulder.

She tried to shrug it off. "I am fine." They walked into the corn field. When Nanny saw Maheeba, she joined them.

Karl patted the goat. "I think I would like living on a farm. Are you happy?"

"Yes. Why do you ask?"

"I want you to know that I am always here for you. If you ever need me."

Maheeba became very uncomfortable, brushing back her hair. She called to the children. "Look what Karl brought. He will fix the wagon so Nanny can pull it."

"Thank you," Tom Tom said as he put the girls into the wagon, and grabbed the handle.

Karl tried to get close to Maheeba but she would walk away and change the subject.

"Look at this large tomato, like my homeland," she said handing it to Karl.

"It's a beaut," Karl said. "It's called a beefsteak. I grew up on a farm."

Nicolas came home and called to the couple. "Get in here you two."

They returned to the house. Karl showed the tomato to Nick. "Isn't it a beauty?"

"It's just a tomato."

"I think it's perfect out here and the corn is the best I've ever eaten. How do you like the farm?" Karl asked Nick.

"It's fine but too remote for me," Nicolas answered. "I miss living in town. This is good for the family. We'll stay here for a few more years. Maheeba is pregnant again."

"Two boys and two girls seems like an ideal family to me," Karl said.

"Not for a Catholic Arab. We have big families."

Maheeba fixed dinner, and served the family. Karl grabbed her arm. "Please join us. We need one more pretty face at the table."

She sat down, folded her arms and said, "Eat, eat."

Two more children, Paul and Jimmy, were born in Weirton. Nicolas seemed pleased, and they were very happy. Maheeba loved the farm. It connected her to her past. "Ime, I am so happy," she thought. "It's like being home with you, but we don't have dates. We have sweet corn. Our vegetables never seem to be as big as the ones that Papa planted. Maybe it was just that I was so little. We have two big cows. We get fresh milk every day. We have six children—four boys. Nicolas seems to enjoy the children, but Tom Tom is always getting into trouble. He is eight years old, and just last week, he was bouncing on the bed, near the window. How many times we tell him not to jump on the bed. He won't listen. He jumped higher, and higher; closer, and closer to the edge. Finally, he bounced so hard that he flew through the glass window, and landed on the roof of the porch. When I heard the crash, my heart stopped. I ran upstairs, and there was Tom Tom lying on a bed of glass in a pool of blood. Marie had to carefully open the window and climbed out to get him. We helped him to the bed and he lay on his stomach, and grabbed the bedpost. He had a big piece of glass in his buttock. I was afraid to pull it out. I couldn't even move. That boy never cried. By the time the doctor came, Tom Tom had lost so much blood, he was weak. I held my son's head while the doctor picked out the glass, and sewed up the cut, without any anesthesia. I gave him some *arak* with water and honey to drink. When

Nicolas got home he went upstairs to see the damage. Tom Tom was still lying on his stomach holding on to the bedpost. 'How many times have I told you not to jump on the bed? See what happens? How dumb are you?' He shouted, without love or sympathy in his voice. He walked over to the window and boarded it up. I didn't know that Nicolas could be so mean."

22

Return to Portsmouth, 1921

"I'm going to sell the farm, "Nicolas announced. "It is too small. We need more room with six children. Jimmy is two, Paul is almost four, and you are expecting another baby."

"Can't we add on?" Maheeba asked.

"I don't want to put any more money in this house. I want to move to town. I like it better there, and my business is growing."

Nicolas sold the farm and moved the family to a big, brick, ostentatious house in Portsmouth. When Maheeba first saw the beautiful, two story house with so many rooms, she stood on the porch, held up both hands and said, "Ime can you see me now? I think your dream for me is coming true. I will miss the farm, it was like home, but this is what Nicolas wants. I hope it makes him happy."

The house had four fireplaces, a big kitchen and dining room with circular windows, and three full baths. The first thing Maheeba noticed was a built in light switch. "Not like the chain," she said, turning the light on and off. The furniture was beautiful and livable—a plush, green velvet couch with needlepoint throw pillows, Chippendale chairs, coffee table, lamps and a china closet. She felt overwhelmed by the space and beauty. "This is like the Sultan's Palace."

Maheeba decorated the kitchen with Papa's crucifix above the door and special utensils from Syria. Among her treasures were: an imported crock, a wooden pestle with a stone mortar, and a sixteen inch round wood paddle with a long handle for baking bread. It was a strange contrast, an oasis in a house full of modern American furniture. An oasis where she could feel comfortable and secure was what she had prayed for. Her dream of a new life was more like living on the farm without the Turks. "I don't understand this society, where women are so independent—working, smoking, equal with men," Maheeba thought. She felt inadequate dealing with this rapidly changing environment. She had never seen change in her culture.

When Nicolas came home, Maheeba, as always, brought a pan of warm soapy water to wash his feet. "No more," he said. "It's too much trouble, and maybe I go out later."

"You don't want to soak your feet?" Maheeba asked. "It will help you to relax."

Nicolas just shook his head and went into the living room to listen to the radio. That was the end of the feet bathing ritual.

Maheeba did her best to adjust to the new life. She and Nadia visited often. "Nicolas hired a woman, Amy, to clean my house." Maheeba said. "He is a good man."

"Tomas said that Nicolas spends too much money, he is foolish."

"My brother will never like my husband," Maheeba said.

By spring Phil was born. "Ime, I have five boys now," Maheeba said, "and another one on the way." But the eighth child was a girl, named Ann.

Nicolas bragged about his children, and enjoyed flaunting his wealth in front of Maheeba's brothers. "You worry too much," Nicolas said to Tomas. "You should buy stock. I made six percent in one week. This is the American dream."

"You, big shot," Tom said, "you act like there's no tomorrow."

Nicolas ignored his relatives, and continued to invest, and spend recklessly. He bought a big Cadillac to take his family on outings, to the park every Sunday or to the lake. Six children could easily crowd into the back. Four could sit on the seat, and then two benches, right and left, attached to the back of the front seat, folded down to seat two more, facing the other passengers. The kids loved it, they would play games.

One Sunday, after a picnic in the park and running races, the family packed up to go home. Maheeba did not count the children, as she usually did, before they climbed into the car. Two of the older boys sat in the front with Nicolas, and Maheba sat in the back with the girls and the younger children. About a mile down the road, she began counting. "Wait, I'm missing someone. Count off." She began, "Number one," Marie called out, "two" Teresa answered, "three" Tom Tom, "four" Mike, "five" Paul, "six" no answer. "Stop, we lost—Jimmy," everyone yelled in unison. Nicolas turned the car around and drove back to the park as fast as he could. It was starting to get dark. Maheeba began to say the rosary out loud and the girls responded. They pulled up to the picnic site and there stood four-year-old Jimmy in his blue striped coveralls and dusty brown shoes, sucking his thumb and trying not to cry. Marie got out of the car and picked up her little brother, "Where were you?" she asked.

"In the bat room," he answered sobbing.

She carried him into the car, sat him on her lap and hugged him. He fell asleep in her arms.

"He was stupid," Nicolas said. "He saw us packing up to leave."

Maheeba made the sign of the cross and said a prayer of thanksgiving. "To lose your child would be a mother's nightmare," she thought, as she looked down at Ann nursing. She remembered the horror, when her sister-in-law's child died accidentally of suffocation while nursing. They were riding in a car and it was cold. Nadia would never get over it.

In 1925 and earlier, parents were concerned about polio, the crippling child disease. There was no prevention and no cure available. Maheeba knew the reality of this illness when a neighbor's child became infected. She felt that her children were at risk. "Nadia what can we do?" Maheeba asked. "We have to protect our children."

"They're not allowed to go swimming or play at the park," Nadia said. "If any more children get sick, they will close the school."

"I asked Nicolas what we should do, and he said, pray like you always do. Maybe he's right. We should pray. I will say a rosary every day."

"I will too."

Both women believed in prayer as a preventative and attributed prayer to the fact that not one of the thirty five children in the family ever got the dreaded disease.

One day there was a knock at the door. "This is a surprise," Maheeba said as she opened the door. Karl was holding a bouquet of flowers.

"I told Nick that I was going to drop by. Here, I brought you some roses."

"Thank you," Maheeba said as she took the flowers. "You're early. Nicolas doesn't get home for another hour."

"I know, but I never get to see you when he's around. You're always in the kitchen."

Maheeba would not make eye contact. She adjusted her apron, and brushed off some flour. "I'll call Nicolas at the office and see if it is okay for you to wait. Come in." She led Karl into the living room, and called Amy to bring some coffee. "Please sit down. I'll be right back."

"Nicolas?" Maheeba recognized his voice on the phone. "Karl is here, he thought you might be home early. Do you want him to come there?"

"Tell him to wait, I'll come right home." Nicolas hung up the phone abruptly, with out saying good bye.

Maheeba placed the receiver in its cradle and joined Karl.

"This is too formal. Can we sit in the kitchen?" Karl asked as he got up.

Maheeba led him into the kitchen, where Jimmy and Paul were playing with building blocks. She offered cheese, olives, bread, and cookies.

"How do you like your new house?" Karl asked as he sat on the floor with the children.

"It is beautiful. I never dreamed it could be so wonderful. I love the flowers. You're kind and thoughtful," Maheeba said. "Why haven't you married? You would make a wonderful father."

"I don't know. Most women aren't honest or good, not like you."

"There are lots of American women to choose from, maybe you're too picky," Maheeba said. "Someone would be lucky to have you."

When Nicolas arrived, Maheeba took the children and went upstairs.

"Why didn't you come by the office?" Nicolas asked Karl.

"I always see you. I wanted to see Maheeba and the kids."

In time, Nicolas sold his shares of the dry goods company, purchased an ice-cream parlor and put the older children to work after school and weekends. As soon as a child was old enough or strong enough to hold a broom to sweep, do dishes, or wipe tables, he went to work. Except Marie, the only one with courage to stand up to her father. "I won't be a soda jerk. It's your store, you run it. I want to go to business school and be a secretary. I'll keep your books but I will also get a job."

Maheeba never disciplined the boys. She would warn, "Wait until you father gets home." But the girls were her responsibility, and she was very critical and strict with them.

"You talk like that to your father?" Maheeba scolded, her eyes flashing and standing right in her daughter's face. "Ladies do not work outside the home unless it's family business. You have big ideas. Why can't you be like Teresa—shy, timid, hard working, no back talk? She's a good Syrian girl. Your dresses are too short. Some day you'll probably be smoking. You are wild, getting out of hand, like"...

"A maverick? I march to my own drummer." Marie was adamant. "When I graduate from eighth grade, I want to go to business school. I already know how to order for the store and keep books. Please, Papa."

"We will talk about it later," Nicolas said as he walked out of the room.

Maheeba followed him. "She needs to get married. She has wild ideas, and you spoil her. That nice family, from Cambridge, the Mourads, they have a good son, he likes Marie."

"You want to arrange a marriage?" "Your daughter is thirteen?"

"Yes, she needs to get married and settle down," Maheeba insisted.

"Never without her consent. My children will not be forced into an arranged marriage. You think like the old country." Nicolas was pacing back and forth. "The world is going crazy. Business is not good. I am losing money. I can't sleep."

"How bad is it?" Maheeba asked. "You never say anything."

"The stock market is going crazy. I don't know what to do."

"You always know what to do. This will pass. Don't you save money for hard times? Like Papa, he stored crops for bad years."

"I wish I had a store house of money," Nicolas said, grabbing his hat. I'm going to the store."

"What about Marie?"

"I will let Marie go to business school. No more discussion."

"At least let me invite the Mourads to visit. We can see what happens. I'll tell them to come for dinner, the next time they are in town."

"Alright! Alright."

23

The Great Depression, 1927

More and more Nicolas would come home from work tired, and drained, as if he were in a dream world. Maheeba would try everything—cook his favorite food, sing, and have the girls dance. "Ime, we are in trouble," she thought. "Nicolas is worried sick. I don't know how to help him. All he talks about is money. He never smiles. We don't make love."

One day Nicolas came home, looking very old. He was bent over, and his shoulders drooped. Maheeba began, as she always did, telling which of the boys misbehaved for him to discipline, but he didn't even hear her. He was pale. "What's wrong? Are you sick?" She shook him to get his attention.

"Don't you listen to the news?" He said, starring straight ahead.

"What news?" Maheeba ran to the living room and turned on the radio. Banks were calling in loans. The stock market had gone down. People who had bought on the margin (paid only part of the purchase price) were unable to sell their stock. The inflated economy was doomed. "What does it mean?" Maheeba asked. "Is it war?"

Nicolas sat in a chair and listened in horror as the voice box predicted his future. "It's the end of the world," he said.

The following days Nicolas was reminded, all too often to "cover the margin," which he did until the money ran out. Like countless others he lost it all. Then the bank began calling, wanting payment. "Why now?" he pleaded, but they were calling in lots of loans.

"Things will be better," Maheeba would say, but reality wouldn't step aside. The necessity for food, clothes for growing children and mounting bills continued to plague the family.

Nicolas faced the fact that he was not making a living, he was barely hanging on. When the money was gone, the rentals and ice-cream parlor—the two most heavily mortgaged investments, were foreclosed. As the economy plunged into a depression, he lost all of his investments. With no assets, he lost his properties;

one by one each was foreclosed. Like dominoes they fell, until the last domino standing was the hotel on Main Street with a $7,000 mortgage.

It was a tall, three story, red brick building, which appeared to grow out of the side of a hill. The back of the building faced Lombardy Heights. The third floor back exit had a long porch and steep steps to the street. The second floor exited under the steps. The front of the building faced Main Street.

A flophouse would be a more accurate description, with its small, dark, individual rooms. The family would move into the third floor, which had five bedrooms, two children to a bed. The living room, with one of the few windows in the building, overlooked Main Street. The only access to the living room was through a bedroom.

The dining room and kitchen were at the opposite end from the living room, and overlooked the back street. The second and third floor each had a small washroom, with only a sink and toilet. It had no window, and no air vent. The bathing facility was a big tin washtub placed in the middle of the kitchen, and water was heated on the stove. Every Saturday, the routine was the same. A sign on the door reserved the room for the boys, and then the girls.

Maheeba's brothers helped the family to move out of their beautiful home to these meager accommodations. They were able to keep their beautiful furniture—the plush green velvet sofa, love seat, hand carved coffee table and Queen Ann chairs. The big round oak dining table with matching chairs stood on a faded, cracked linoleum floor. The glass enclosed oak china closet was a perfect show case for the family crystal.

A cedar chest held Maheeba's treasures of gold jewelry and coins, her dowry. Here she kept her wedding dress and Ime's things, linking the present to the past. Everything looked out of place housed in such dilapidated surroundings. The second floor had a few boarders. A large room in the front was rented out to a bookie for off track betting.

The bedrooms opened on to a mezzanine, a square, mirroring the perimeter of the skyline above, allowing the sunlight to shine through to the second floor. The children could look over the railing and watch the men coming and going after visiting the bookies. They would play a guessing game, "Look at that short man. I'll bet he has a tall wife and stands on a chair to kiss her," Ann said laughing.

Phil would add, "That skinny man probably has a fat wife who orders him around."

It was the beginning of the end for Nicolas, financially and emotionally. He had his first of a series of nervous breakdowns. "I wonder," Maheeba thought, "was it the sudden loss of his fortune or the fact that he will have to depend on my brothers, or both? How could this happen? Just twenty years after Nicolas and I met on Ellis Island, we are lost in America. Is this the promise of the new world?"

Nicolas' recovery was gradual and emotionally painful. He had all of the symptoms of severe depression, a deep uncertainty that led to indecision about everything, even what clothes to wear. He wanted to seclude himself from people, and the family. Maheeba sensed his overwhelming doubt about himself and his abilities. He even questioned her every move. She did not understand his behavior, and wondered if it was the evil eye.

After six months Nicolas pulled himself together, and took over the Pastime Pool Room on the first floor of the hotel and put the children to work. They managed, poorly, but managed. Maheeba's bywords were, "make do and always pay cash". She made over dresses, shirts, blouses and trousers. She appliquéd patches on clothes fifty years before the designer jean rage.

24

An Arranged Marriage, 1927

When Marie graduated from the eighth grade, she refused to work in the ice-cream parlor. Instead she studied at a business school and got a job bookkeeping at a brewery. She was tall, poised, well dressed, self confident, stubborn, and intelligent. She was the first Syrian woman to work outside of her family business. Her free spirit kept her at odds with her mother.

"I worry about Marie," Maheeba told Nadia. "She has too many American men giving her gifts. We need to find her a good Syrian man."

"What does Nicolas say?" Nadia asked.

"He says no arranged marriage. She is fourteen now. I want her to meet Joseph Mourad, a nice Syrian man from Cambridge."

"Maheeba, this isn't the old country," Nadia said. "Nicolas is right."

"I just want to see her married," Maheeba said. "I invited the Mourads to dinner next week. We will see what happens."

The family included Joseph, a very nice looking young man of eighteen, and his mother, a stern opinionated old woman with a frozen frown on her face. She looked as if she hadn't smiled in years. She was dressed in black. The entourage included an aunt, a rigid, frigid old maid and an unmarried older sister. This family unit had all the dynamics to produce a dysfunctional, neurotic offspring.

Before dinner, the young couple went for a walk.

"They make a handsome pair, don't they?" Maheeba commented.

"It's no concern of mine. How much is the dowry?" Mrs. Mourad asked.

"Mr. Thomas is very generous and will give money for the children to set up housekeeping."

"I will be losing my son and he is a source of income," Mrs. Mourad said. "What will I get?"

"Nothing. My husband feels that both families should mutually approve the marriage, but refuses to consider a pre arrangement. The children must agree freely on their own, no dowry."

"You cheat a poor old woman out of her money? I want my son to live in Cambridge."

"My daughter will refuse. That must be my husband now." Maheeba went to greet Nicolas and said, "The mother is an old biddy. Marie will put her in her place. It's just what she deserves. I like Joseph."

Taking off his coat, Nicolas said, "I never liked her." "She's hard as nails. I use to provide goods for their small store. She always complained and wanted more. I don't know about that family. Let's just get through tonight." They went into the living room and greeted their guests. Nicolas was a gracious host, and dinner went well, even though Mrs. Mourad tried to talk about an arrangement. He refused to discuss it, saying, "We will see what happens."

After they left, Maheeba asked Marie, "How did you like Joseph? He would make a good husband. They want you to visit them. We can all go."

"He is a wimp, a mama's boy. I don't want to get married yet."

Maheeba persisted, relentlessly, talking about Joseph all the time. She told Marie how wonderful it would be to have a home of her own, a family, and a big wedding. Times were hard and the economy did not improve. Finally, at fourteen, Marie consented to be married.

She agreed to marry in the Orthodox Church, to please her in-laws. The wedding was small. Marie wore Maheeba's wedding gown. With a few alterations, she was just as beautiful a bride as her mother had been. Joseph gave her a stunning gold necklace on their wedding night. Marie continued to work at the Brewery and Joseph got a job at a men's store. They rented a small apartment in Wheeling.

The first month went well, and then Joseph became moody. He called his mother often, and complained about missing his family. "Mom," Marie said, "Joseph goes to Cambridge most weekends, with or without me. This is not a marriage made in heaven."

"He loves his mother. That's a good thing," Maheeba said.

On their three month anniversary, Joseph told Marie, "My mother called and she wants to see me tomorrow."

"That's Wednesday. You can't take off work, neither can I. Besides I have a doctor's appointment tomorrow. You know that I have morning sickness. If you wait until Saturday at noon we can both go."

"Okay, I'll wait until Saturday." Joseph then followed Marie into the kitchen and watched her fix dinner.

The next day Marie went to the doctor, who confirmed her suspicions. She was pregnant. Hearing the good news, she stopped at the store to get a steak and an apple pie for a celebration dinner. When she got home, the house was dark and cold. She put down the groceries and called for Joseph. He wasn't there but she found his note. "Went to my mother's, I'll be back by Friday." Marie tore up the note, grabbed the food and took the bus to her parent's house.

"What's wrong?" Maheeba asked, when she saw her daughter. "Where's Joseph?"

"At his mother's," Marie snapped.

"You should be with him."

"Mom, I'm working, I had a doctor's appointment today and he agreed to wait until Saturday. Don't defend him."

"His mother must be sick. What did your doctor say?"

"I'm pregnant, and where is my husband? Celebrating with his family. It won't work. It's over."

"Don't say that. It takes time to adjust and now you will be a family." Maheeba took the groceries from her daughter. "Sit down, I'll fix some coffee."

Joseph arrived home Friday evening to an empty apartment. All he found was the torn note. He went down the hall to the pay phone to call but Marie would not talk to him. He waited up until midnight, and then went to bed. The next day he went to his in-laws house to see his wife.

"Come in, I'll fix you something to eat," Maheeba said greeting him as though nothing were wrong.

Marie was quiet all through dinner. The younger siblings looked from one to the other, waiting for an argument. After dinner Maheeba said, "You two talk, we will clean up."

Marie agreed to go home with her husband and try again to make the marriage work. Life was tolerable, and they even had some good times. She quit work in her sixth month and was advised not to travel. Joseph continued to visit his mother alone. He was in Cambridge when his son was born. Rushing back he missed the delivery. Marie was disappointed but never complained. They named the baby Joey.

On Joey's first birthday, Marie returned home from shopping. She was greeted with the sound of her son crying, hysterically. "Joseph, Joseph, where are you?"

She went into the bedroom and found her baby alone, in his crib, crying. "My poor darling, don't cry. It's okay." She picked the baby up. "Let's go find Daddy."

Joseph was nowhere to be found. The baby's piggy bank was broken. The shattered pieces were scattered all over the dresser. Not only had he deserted them, he had also stolen the baby's money, leaving just a note, that read "sorry."

Marie kissed the baby and comforted him. "My Joey, it's okay, Mommy is home now. We'll go visit Tata. Your diaper is a mess. How long have you been laying in this?" She bathed and dusted him with talcum powder, then changed his clothes. She unbuttoned her blouse, sat in the rocking chair and nursed her son. He was contented in her arms. His little hands kneaded his mother's breast and he fell asleep. Marie put her son in his crib, then went down the hall to the pay phone and called her father. "Dad, this is Marie, come and get me. Joseph ran out on us again, but this time he left the baby alone. Please come quick."

"I'll be there in a few minutes. I'll bring Paul with me."

She hung up before she started crying. Consumed with anger, she screamed, "My son left alone and frightened! How could he do this? I'll never go back to him! I can make it on my own."

By the time Nicolas arrived, she had everything packed and sitting in the hallway. "What happened?" he asked.

"When I got home," Marie said, "Joseph was gone, with Joey's money. The baby was wet, dirty, hungry and crying. He abandoned us and endangered our child."

"How long were you gone?" Paul asked, frightened by the scene.

"About three hours," Marie said.

The picture of his nephew, alone and scared, would never leave Paul and he would never forgive his brother-in-law.

"Take those bags and things there," she said pointing. "We can get the rest later. I'm not coming back. This is it." She bundled up her son, and Paul loaded up the car. They took what they could and headed for Portsmouth.

When they arrived, Maheeba reached for her grandson. "Joey, you get bigger every day. Where is Joseph?"

"At his mother's. Where else!"

"Why didn't you go with him?"

"Mom," Marie said, "he went while I was shopping and left the baby alone for hours. "He deserted us."

"Why didn't he bring Joey to me? What is wrong with a father who can leave his baby alone?"

"Alleluia, mom sees the light," Marie said, raising her hands in jubilation.

Joseph tried to call Marie at the Pastime Pool room, Michael answered and said, "She won't talk to you and you aren't welcome here."

Joseph tried to call several times and finally went to Portsmouth with his mother. They went to the Thomas's house. Maheeba, the only member of the family who would welcome them, answered the door. "Marie won't be home until noon, but come in." She led them to the living room, where Ann and Phil were playing blocks, and Joey was waking up from a nap. Maheeba picked up the baby and offered him to Joseph. "This is your Papa. Come into the kitchen and I'll get some coffee."

Mrs. Mourad never made a loving gesture toward her grandson, "Joseph wants his family back. We will take them to Cambridge."

"We will wait for Marie," Maheeba said as she poured coffee and offered some bread, cheese and dried fruit. She took the baby from his father and cradled him in her arms.

Within the hour, Marie arrived with her sister Teresa. Her brow over her dark eyes was furrowed in a frown. With out a word she took her child and stood facing the enemy.

"You needn't have come. It's over. I'll never go back."

"You can't do that. You were married in the church. What reason?" Mrs. Mourad said, getting up from the table.

"What about desertion?" Marie said looking at her husband. "You endangered our child, leaving him alone, God knows how long it might have been."

"I'm sorry," Joseph said as he walked over to his wife. "I know it was wrong. I don't know why I did it. I won't do it again. I promise."

"I can't take that chance, for Joey's sake. You'd better leave now." Marie then walked out of the room, without saying good-bye.

The next day, Marie went to see the priest at St. Anthony's Church. Father Whitman had baptized her and officiated at her parents wedding. "Father, I want to know if my marriage can be annulled. I was married in the Orthodox Church. My husband deserted my baby and me."

"The Church recognizes the Orthodox marriage. That's not grounds for an annulment. Were you forced into the marriage?" Father asked, inviting her to sit down.

"No, I was talked into it. I was only fourteen."

"Did he want children? Did he refuse to have more or allow them to be raised Roman Catholic? These are reasons for an annulment," Father said, walking up to Marie.

A feeling of hopelessness came over her. "Father, I can't lie. We never discussed it. I believe in my heart that he wouldn't object to more children or raising them Catholic."

"Perhaps you should try again to make your marriage work," Father said. "Let's pray for guidance."

Marie slid to her knees and Father placed his hands on her head and prayed. Together they said the Lords Prayer.

"Thank you Father, I know what I must do."

"You will return to your husband?"

"No, I'll file for a divorce."

On her way home, she stopped at the courthouse to get the divorce papers.

When she arrived home, Teresa was anxiously waiting for the news. "What happened? Can you get an annulment?"

Without a word, Marie handed her sister the papers. "Oh, I'm sorry," she said, reaching out, to hug her. "What will mom say?"

Hearing the voices, Maheeba walked into the room. "What are you going to do?"

"Get a divorce."

In Syria only husbands could apply. No one Maheeba knew ever divorced. "Dear Allah. What did Father say? Can you stay in the church?"

"Yes. It's okay Mom. I won't be excommunicated. I just can't remarry and that's not a problem."

Joseph never contested the divorce and never saw his son again. Marie did not ask for alimony or child support.

One day, while Marie was preparing food for her son, Maheeba walked in.

"What are you doing?"

"I'm fixing dinner for Joey, this is a ricer. I cooked the meat rare, put it in this, press down and the juice comes out, over rice. I don't have to chew it for the baby. They even sell baby food in jars."

"That's rice? It is so sticky."

"It's soft for the baby, this isn't a cooking contest."

Marie's determination to be her own person labeled her a free spirit. Any time, every time a woman in the family was assertive, Maheeba would say, in despair, "You are just like Marie."

Marie continued to work and was promoted. Teresa was hired at the Warwick china factory. The younger children worked as delivery boys and ran errands.

25

I am number nine, 1929

At dawn, January 4, 1929, Mom carefully made her way to Marie's bedroom. The Christmas tree was still standing in the living room. It was more dead than alive with a puddle of needles at its feet. "It's cold," Mom thought. She looked into the pot belly stove and saw a faint beacon of light. One or two coals had survived the night. She stoked the fire, and then continued to her daughter's room.

"Marie," she whispered. "It's time, get up, we have to go to the hospital. Wake up Teresa."

Mom made her way back to her room to get ready. Her legs felt too weak to support her body. "Help!" she yelled as she slid back into bed.

The children rushed to their mother's side. "The baby is coming! Quick, get something." Marie ordered her siblings, with the force of a drill sergeant leading a combat mission. "Teresa! Put water on the stove. Get a sheet and towels." Her baby began to cry. "Get Joey," she yelled at Mike.

Relying on instinct, Marie put a sheet under her mother. She could see the baby coming. "Jimmy, go to Wilson's and tell them Mom's delivering now. Hurry up."

Jimmy put on his boots, coat and hat, and ran toward the mortuary. Mother Nature had beautified the town with a white blanket of snow. The ice on the boxed tree in front of the City Bank sparkled. Fred, a city worker was shoveling snow from the steps. It was quiet; the Streetcar had not yet left the station. *Wilson's Funeral Home* was just a block away. As Jimmy crossed through the doorway, he grabbed an icicle and sucked on it. "Mr. Wilson, come quick. My Mom is having a baby."

"I'll get my coat," he said. "You can ride back with me."

There were only two emergency vehicles in the town—the fire truck and the hearse.

Dad had not come home all night. Mom talked about him, and how he had changed. His behavior had become more erratic. He was seldom happy. His constant accusations of unfaithfulness, and violent temper tantrums were more frequent. "This was not a child conceived in love and tenderness," Mom told Nadia later. "Not like the first born. Nicolas just took possession of what was his. Even the sexual act wasn't lovemaking, it was rape."

"Momma, you okay?" Teresa asked.

"Yes, everything will be fine," Mom said. "Allah, help us," she pleaded silently. Dad had forced himself on mom. He was mean drunk, violent, and he hurt her, but she still loved him. She would have welcomed him to her bed for a kiss, a touch, any sign of affection, not anger and rage. What did she do wrong, she wondered. Why couldn't she make him happy?

Now nine months later, I arrived into this world, ready or not. I was born, there in the bedroom. Within minutes I slid through the birth canal onto the towel Marie was holding, and was completely silent. Marie held me upside down, patted my back, and then I cried.

"How did I know to do that?" Marie said.

"Cut the cord." Mom said faintly.

"No, Mom, I can't." Marie wrapped me, cord and all in a blanket. Then she turned to Teresa and said, "Bring me a wet cloth to wipe the baby's face."

I sucked my hand, and closed my eyes as Marie carried me over to her eighteen-month-old son. "This is your aunt," she said, bending over for Joey to see. He reached out and touched my tiny hand.

Soon help arrived, a hearse and a driver to take us to the hospital. They wrapped my mother in blankets, put her on a stretcher and carried her to the black carriage. The smell of fresh flowers permeated the air. Mom opened her eyes and saw a big wreath standing at her feet, with a wide red ribbon that read, Rest in Peace. "I hope this is a good omen," she thought.

"Take care of Joey," Marie said. "I'll be back later. Teresa, call Uncle Hashar and tell him what happened." Looking down at the sleeping bundle in her arms, she said, "Someday I will tell you the story of your birth. We are the Alpha and the Omega, the beginning and the end of the Thomas family."

I was the ninth child, and Dad was nowhere to be found. He was gone a lot, missing for days at a time.

"Where is the Father?" The doctor asked.

"Working," Mom replied.

The doctor checked the mother and child, and we were both fine. "You did a good job," he said to Marie. "I'll have to teach you to cut the umbilical cord. You would make a good mid-wife."

We stayed at the hospital until evening, and then went home with Uncle Hashar.

"What name shall we put on the birth certificate?" A nurse asked.

"I don't know," Mom answered. "My husband never talked about it."

"Nine months, and you have no idea?"

"He works a lot."

All were discharged with a copy of the certificate that read, "Thomas, unnamed, female, eight pounds two ounces." I don't know how or when they came up with the name Ellen, but it had to be a Saint's name.

Dad arrived home that evening, and seeing his ninth child, he said jubilantly, "Get out the *arak*, we'll celebrate."

My first Easter was memorable, not that I remember it, but my siblings talked about it often. It was the last big holiday that Dad was with us, and he was happy. Dad was taking an anti-depressant, and it worked, as long as he controlled his alcohol consumption. That morning, like so many Sundays when Dad was his former self, he woke his children singing, "Good morning sunshine, you shine so soon, you scare the stars and shine with the moon."

"Oh no! Dad, do you have to be so cheery in the morning?" Paul mumbled as he pulled the pillow over his head.

"It's Easter, we have to go to church." Jimmy climbed over his brother to get out of bed.

Mom was already in the kitchen, making hot chocolate for the little ones. No coffee, everyone over the age of seven had to fast for communion.

Teresa, who shared a room with Marie and her son Joey, came into the kitchen.

"Can I help, Mom?"

"Get Ann and Phil dressed for church."

"Mike, get up." Tom Tom shook his sleeping brother. "Do you have the egg ready?"

"It's okay. Get out of here!"

"What's going on?" Paul, who shared the bed with Mike, asked.

"Mike boiled his egg in sand," Tom Tom said. "It'll be strong."

"What?"

"He stood the egg up in sand so all the stuff went to the bottom. We will win the contest with the Bakeers."

Mike dressed quickly and went into the kitchen. On the top shelf of the cupboard he retrieved his coveted egg. "Mom, this is a champion. We will win the egg fight."

"You didn't color it."

"It's white like the good guys."

Dad walked up to his son. "Let's try it. Hit my egg."

"Yesss! The mighty white warrior crushed his first victim," Mike said.

Dad turned his egg over, "Now I hit you."

Giving himself every advantage, Mike molded his fingers, gently but firmly, cradling his prize like a baby chick, and exposing only the tip. With the expertise of a sharp shooter, Dad hit the target as hard as he could—shattering his own egg.

This ritual was repeated throughout the family, eliminating each one until the last surviving egg.

"It's my turn, Brother. Let's see you knock me out," Marie said, holding a pretty pink egg, ready for combat.

"Okay, Sis." Mike carefully and skillfully took aim and hit the target right on the tip.

Everyone stared in disbelief. "Your egg broke," Marie said triumphantly.

"Turn it over and hit me."

"I win," Marie said. "You will have to enter the contest with a pink egg."

"No it can't be." Mike picked up another egg and another, until he destroyed the entire three dozen. "We have to fight our cousins, with a pink egg. What a joke."

"You better win. I bet money," Dad said.

After church the family had breakfast, while Mom packed up a picnic lunch. Like most Sundays they met their cousins at Olgelby Park for a family outing.

Mom had prepared meat pies, *kibby,* eggplant, rolled grape leaves and Syrian bread. Nadia brought stuffed squash, *tabouli,* green beans, rice, and hamburgers to grill. Uncle Hashar brought drinks.

By one o'clock, they had all gathered at site twenty-three. While the women fixed lunch, the men and children gathered around to watch the big egg fight event. As in medieval history, the battle would be determined by two opposing warriors. Joe Bakeer was the champion for his family and Mike was the Thomas's Prince Valiant. The challengers entered the ring.

"Any more bets, before I take out the Pink Lady?" Joe asked, holding up his dark reddish black egg with a cross painted on it.

"We'll flip a coin to see who hits first," Dad said, tossing a quarter in the air.

"Heads!" Mike called.

Dad stepped aside and let the coin hit the ground. "Heads it is."

"Prepare to die, Cousin." Mike kissed his egg and took aim.

The mighty Pink Lady crushed the Black Knight.

"My turn." Joe turned his egg over and took aim. He rammed his prize into the opponent's egg.

Mike held up his unblemished prize. "The Pink Lady wins. Pay up you losers."

Dad hugged his son. "About time we win."

"All this trouble for one little egg fight," Mom said.

"I know," Nadia said. "They do it every year. Nicolas is in a good mood. Is he better?"

"Today is good. He has to take his medicine and not drink. If he gets drunk, he goes crazy, breaks things, and yells. I wish he would work or do something. He use to be busy all the time, thinking of new things to do. I think he forgot how smart he is. He's afraid to do anything. All we can do is pray."

Uncle Tom walked over to the women. "We eat now," he said as he picked up the hamburgers to grill.

After lunch, the older children gathered up the younger ones to go swimming. I fell asleep on my mother's lap. "Be careful and watch the babies real good," Mom yelled.

The women cleaned up, put food away and set out watermelon and pastries for dessert. By seven o'clock, they started to pack up to leave. "It's getting dark, the park will close soon. Get the little ones," Mom called to the older children.

That was March, and the economy, with it's up and down swings, seemed to be surviving. No way could the Thomas family have anticipated the brewing storm that brought black October. Seven months later, the country plunged into its darkest hour, Wall Street collapsed. People, who rode the wave of prosperity, thought it would never end. Many corporate heads, who invested everything in stock, committed suicide. It was the worst disaster in the history of the United States.

26

The worst of times, 1930

The stock market crash in 1929, threw my father deeper into depression. It seemed that he, and the country were in a downward spiral. The next few months were difficult. Dad's trips were more frequent and more extensive. His behavior was more erratic, with extreme mood swings of anger and depression. He drank a lot. He was admitted to the hospital in Pittsburgh for a nervous break down. Sometimes when he was home, life was pleasant. We were like a normal family. Other times, he would be angry, violent; we never knew what would trigger the rage. Mom tried to believe that his angry, aberrant moods were signs of exhaustion.

One day, Dad came home in a good mood. He had bought a Ford sedan, not new, but in good condition. Handing the keys to Teresa, he said, "This is for your sixteenth birthday. You've been driving since you were thirteen. It's time you had a car."

"She shouldn't drive. I know she is your favorite, you spoil her. Girls get into trouble that way." Mom protested.

"None of the boys have a car of there own," Teresa said, "why me?" Since Tom Tom was unable to drive, Mike should have been the first.

"Women should not be allowed to drive, it is unheard of." Mom complained, every time Dad took Teresa out. But he exercised his right as a man to make decisions based on the absolute power of masculinity. No one ever questioned Dad's actions nor complained about his behavior.

"I'll take you in to get your license." Mike told Teresa.

A week later, Mom rode with Teresa to Karl's garage to check out the car.

Seeing them getting out of the car, Karl stopped what he was doing and walked over. "Maheeba, Teresa, how are you? Is this the newest addition?" He pulled the blanket away from my face, "She's beautiful, just like her sister. You have the prettiest girls in town."

"Thank you, this is Ellen."

Putting his hand on Mom's he said, "How are you? How is Nick?"

"We are both fine. Nicolas bought Teresa the car for her birthday and we need to have it checked out."

"So this is your wheels," he said, walking around the car. "It looks good, girl. Get in and start it up." Karl listened to the engine, and then looked under the hood. "Sounds great, it purrs like a kitten. Leave it here and we'll change the oil and clean her up."

"Thanks, Karl. Can you believe that Dad gave it to me? I just got my license."
"Mom, I need to get something at the drug store next door."

"Go, and get some baby powder too. I'll wait here while Karl finishes up. If that's okay?"

Karl called to a mechanic and told him to change the oil. "Can I get you something?" He pulled a chair over for Mom to sit down, "I'm glad you stayed. How is Nick, really? I hear so many things. The boys are disgusted with him. Did he ever hurt you?"

Mom dropped her eyes, not to betray her husband.

"I can still kick his ass."

"No, please," Mom pleaded. "He is sick. His sons have given up on him. He must be hurting. Give it time."

Teresa returned from the store.

"I give your car a clean bill of health," Karl said to Teresa while helping Maheeba into the car.

"Thank you for your support. What do we owe you?"

"How about dinner? Tell Nick he owes me a visit."

"We are taking the baby to the Carmelite Monastery for the cloister nuns to bless and dedicate her to God. In the old country it would be the ceremony of purification."

"I would like to see that," Karl said. "Do they let you in? Can you see them?"

"No, we will put her on the wheel, where we put food and send her to the sisters."

I began to cry. "She's hungry. I'll have to nurse her. Come for Sunday dinner. First, join us for the nine o'clock Mass at the Mt. Carmel church. Then we'll go to the Monastery. Later we eat and celebrate. Good bye," Mom said as she unbuttoned her blouse.

"See you Sunday at church. Bye for now." He shut the car door and waved.

After church, they walked to the Monastery. There was a big heavy wheel, like a grinding mill, laying flat on its side. It had individual baskets secured to it. Mom rang the bell, which called the nuns attention.

"Yes, my child," A Sister's voice could be heard.

"Sister, I'm Mabel Thomas. Will you bless my daughter?"

"Mabel, how good it is to hear your voice again. You're one of our regular providers. Another baby? God has blessed you abundantly."

Mom placed me on a basket and bundled me up. "Her name is Ellen."

Teresa and Jimmy put the groceries—bread, coffee, butter, jam and canned goods in the other baskets. Karl contributed a big bag of fruit.

They turned the wheel. Sister picked me up, and prayed loud enough for the family to hear. Other Nuns joined in chanting. Then Sister put me back into the basket and returned me to my waiting family. "You have another beautiful girl. Thank you for coming and God bless you."

Four difficult years later, the Thomas family continued to struggle. Dad had owned five 'slum' houses next to the railroad track. When Mom collected rent, she would take cookies for the tenants. After the bank foreclosed, she continued to deliver homemade bread and jelly.

"I don't want you to go there. It is dangerous," Dad commanded as he took the basket from her arm. "It's not a good place for Ellen."

"Don't forbid me to go," she pleaded. "God will take care of us."

Dad slammed the basket down on the table and walked out of the room. "Do what you want."

I was about four years old, but I remember the arguments well. The old houses and the poor people would forever be imprinted in my memory.

Mom picked up the basket. She no longer listened or trusted Dad's judgment as she had before. "He is not always right," she thought. She made the sign of the cross, took me by the hand and walked out of the house to catch a streetcar.

We arrived at the first dilapidated house, one with a broken gate, cracked windows, weeds and garbage in the yard. "These must be the poorest of the poor," I thought. "Who are these people?"

In contrast, I noticed expensive, neglected toys lying about. A bicycle and dolls were rusting and dirty in the yard. "I wish I had those toys," I thought. "I would never let my doll get dirty."

An unshaven man, in a torn, dirty undershirt, answered the door. When he saw us, he smiled, exposing the spaces in his mouth where teeth should have been. "You never forget us. Sometimes I think you are the only one in the world that remembers."

Mom gave him his share of the food. "God bless you," she said. Then we went next door. After distributing all her goods, Mom took me by the hand and started for home.

"Mama, why do they have a doll and a bike?" I asked, tugging on her dress. "We don't have a bike."

"They are on Welfare and stores donate toys." Sensing I didn't understand, Mom continued. "Their Papa isn't working and they don't have money for food."

"But they don't like their toys."

"I don't know why they don't take care of their things," Mom said, pulling me along to catch the streetcar. I tell you children to keep things nice and they will last."

Bread lines and food distribution centers grew as the country slipped deeper into the Depression. So many jobless men took to the streets, going from house to house asking for work in exchange for food. Our house was marked with an X, the sign that this household was generous and they would not turn you away hungry.

Early every Saturday morning, Mom would bake from fifty to a hundred loaves of bread. She would lay a white sheet on the floor of the kitchen. Then she would toss the fresh baked Syrian bread on this gigantic cloth platter. The aroma of fresh bread welcomed the children to breakfast.

"Syrian wheaties," Phil said as he rolled up his buttered bread and dipped it into his cup of milk, laced with a little bit of coffee. "It's our breakfast of Champions."

Daily, Mom also made a huge pot of potato soup, just for the poor. Almost everyday someone would come by hungry, with the same sad story, "Can you spare some food?" Sometimes there were families.

On the back porch she had a long wooden table with benches on each side, to service her soup kitchen. In the winter she would invite the drifters into the house.

Often she found a block of cheese, bags of rice, beans, butter, and other surplus food left at her doorstep from someone she had befriended. Sometimes I thought it was her repentance—not for herself, but for Dad.

27

Being poor and not knowing it, 1933

The economy worsened. Like a cancer it metastasized, touching every walk of life. If our family qualified for surplus food, Mom would never know because Dad would not apply. It didn't matter to Mom, at least on the outside. She refused to think that we were poor. "With family we are rich, we just don't have money. I know that things will get better," Mom said. "We are lucky. There are people worse off than us."

She continued to sing in the kitchen, while cooking, and the family never went hungry. There was always a pan of homemade chocolate syrup on the stove to mix with milk. The youngest boys, Paul and Phil, would walk the two blocks to the Dairy, carrying their gallon jugs to purchase milk at twenty cents a gallon.

On Fridays the menu was always the same. According to Mom it was the specialty of the house—potato soup, mashed potatoes and French fries. "This is the proper way to eat. You dip your French fry into the mashed potatoes," Mom would say as she demonstrated. It was a big hit with us kids.

Mom not only cooked for us, she handled all of Dad's responsibilities. We were taught to be competitive with strong work ethics. "You must be the best you can be," Dad would say. "Everyone thinks Arabs are lazy."

"Always do a little more. Hard work won't hurt you. Your boss will notice." Mom would add. The children proudly gave Mom their earnings. "Look, Paul made twenty-five cents today, delivering groceries for Mr. Helil. I'll bet you can do better tomorrow. See how easy it is to make money if you try?" she would say encouraging the other siblings.

It was a struggle to save even a dime to treat the children to a movie. So Mom said, "If you earn a dollar, you can keep ten cents to go to the show."

Jimmy at age twelve went to the movie theater next door, and asked the manager, Mr. Taylor, if he could sweep and clean out the place. "You won't have to pay me, unless you want to," he said. "Just let my family see the shows free."

"Five days a week. After ten p.m., you will have to sweep with a broom. On Saturday, they vacuum." The manager paused. "Okay kid, it's a deal. Shake."

Every night, Mom would wake Jimmy up before eleven o'clock. "It's time to sweep out the theater," she would say.

Jimmy would climb over his brother to get out of bed. Sometimes he even slept with his clothes on. He slipped on shoes and socks and was off to work. In exchange for his services, everyone in the family received a pass—good for all day, everyday.

Mom enjoyed the *Cliff hanger* series. One of the kids would always tell her when it was time, and she would leave the youngest children in an older child's care and go to the movies. She would always return in about an hour, like clockwork.

Jimmy was a good worker and did a little extra by dusting when needed. This earned him one dollar a week. Before Christmas, Mr. Taylor approached Jimmy, "Would you like to make a little Christmas money?" he asked.

"Yes." Jimmy answered eagerly. "What do I have to do?"

"I have a Christmas Tree lot at the gas station. I could use you to work on Saturday. You would help customers pick out a tree and put it on their car. I'll give you five cents a tree."

"What time?" Jimmy asked, putting his broom away.

"Nine, nine thirty. It gets busy around ten."

"Shake. It's a deal." Jimmy held out his hand to seal the agreement. When he got home, he happily told Mom about the new job.

"I'm so proud of you. Maybe he will give us a good price on a tree."

The next morning, Jimmy got up, dressed, ate, took a lunch, walked the mile to the tree lot and arrived early.

By five o'clock, Mr. Taylor walked over to Jimmy, who was sweeping up tree needles, "See a tree you like? You can pick out a tree for your family and it will be my Christmas present to you. Here." He handed him a dollar bill.

"It wasn't that many trees, more like fourteen," Jimmy said, not reaching for the money.

"It's a bonus, for being such a good worker."

"Thank you," he said, taking the money. My Mom sure will be pleased. If it's okay with you, I'll pick out a tree and go home."

Jimmy, with Mr. Taylor's help, tied a rope around the base of the tree and strapped it across his chest like a harness. He then dragged it home in the snow. It was getting dark, so he took a back street. When he arrived home he pulled it, step by step up to the back porch. He opened the door and yelled for help. Mike and Tom Tom untied their brother as Mom held the little children back, out of the way. They stood the tree up, and the kids began to laugh.

"It's stripped in the back. Not one needle left," Mike announced as he turned the tree around to expose the bare back.

Jimmy held back tears as he looked at the pitiful sight.

"It's perfect for the corner in the living room. It makes the front more full and we have just enough decorations," Mom exclaimed as she hugged and kissed her son. "Thank you for the beautiful tree." Then she turned to Mike, and hit him lightly on the side of his head. "If it was up to you, we wouldn't have a tree."

They leaned the tree against the porch railing until they could build a stand. The tree was decorated with painted walnut shells glued together to make ornaments. Sucker sticks made crosses. Chains were made from cranberries and popcorn. There were a few ornaments and lights which had been purchased years before. The tree would remain in the house until the Epiphany, January sixth. Gifts were given on that day in honor of the Three Kings. Mom had a present for each child to open on that day. It was a handkerchief for the boys with their initial embroidered on it and ribbons for the girls and an orange.

"In Syria," Mom said, "We only got a gift on the Epiphany, not Christmas." Mom kept alive the customs of the old country. The girls would help Mom make *Zalabee* which signifies sweet and everlasting life. She fried the doughnut cakes and sprinkled them with sugar. "My mother would baptize the dough," Mom said. "Just like Father baptized you. We would tie the dough in a white cloth and take it to the well. There we would dip it in water and chant, 'in the name of the Father, Son and Holy Ghost.' After three days, the dough rose without yeast. Like a miracle."

In the spring Mom took us children up Lombardy Heights, beyond Aunt Nadia's house, to unclaimed land, and pick dandelions. Late summer the outing was repeated to pick blackberries and elderberries. For the occasion, Mom would make a batch of cookies with one cookie twice as large as the others. Along with the treat she took sandwiches so we could picnic. After lunch we would play and roll down the hill.

Handing us each a bag, she would say, "Everyone has to pick to earn a cookie. The one who picks the most, gets the big cookie." We accepted the challenge and worked as hard as we could.

On our way home we often stopped at Uncle Tom's house to visit and play with our cousins. Aunt Nadia would treat us to chocolate milk.

Hashar's daughter, Cora, married Vince Rossi, an Italian. When they visited, Vince would treat the younger children to polenta. He would spread the cooked, thick cornmeal mush on the enamel oblong table. Then he covered it with his home made spaghetti sauce, topped with grated cheese.

Pulling chairs up to the table, he handed each one a fork. He would invite the children to eat right off of the table. "The one who makes the best design, not sloppy, wins a sucker."

As everyone ate, we would shield our masterpiece with the other arm to protect it from being copied. Joey, my nephew, won once. He outlined his 'house' with the back of his fork, and then ate the sides to leave an extended roof. He ate a window and door, even a chimney. It was ingenious, and he shared the sucker he had won with me, according to the pact we made.

Phil, the youngest and the shortest of the Thomas boys, nicknamed "Pee Wee" was the personification of "Dennis the Menace". He was also the school clown. He told me that when he was a freshman in high school, he studied the vent to the furnace in his classroom. "If, when the fan comes on," he said, "I throw something down the vent; it will hit the fan blade and shoot out of the vent." To test his theory, he took three ball bearings from an old roller skate.

"The next day," Phil said, "I waited for the furnace to go on. When I heard the fan and felt the warm air, I tossed the balls through the vent. They hit the blade with a noise that only metal on metal could make. The balls were tossed in the air, fell back on the fan and tossed up again, a continuously deafening cycle. The sound was horrendous. The students jumped out of their seats, screaming, that the furnace wais going to explode. The teacher ordered everyone out side. The entire school had to be evacuated. We stood in the cold until the janitor could turn off the furnace. I was sent home. After a week, the principal called Dad, and told him to send me back to school. Dad wanted to keep me home to work, but it's the law, so I went back."

I loved to listen to my brother. He was never boring.

When Mom was canning tomatoes, she put the rotten ones in a basket and told Phil to throw them in the garbage.

"Come on, we'll play a game," he beckoned to me. I followed him out to the back porch. "Now, this is the way it goes. You stand down here at the foot of the stairs, and get the whole basket of tomatoes, except one." He positioned me in the line of fire and took one big rotten tomato. He climbed to the top of the steps and stood on the porch near the kitchen door. "When I count three," he put up three fingers to demonstrate, "you get to throw all of them and I have to dodge, yike." He danced around to make me laugh. "Ready? One," he lowered one finger, "two…." He threw his tomato, hit me in the face and ducked inside the house.

"Mommy, Mommy!" I stood there crying as the red, mushy seeds slid down my face.

Mom and Ann ran outside to the source of the wailing. Ann laughed. Mom pulled off her apron and wiped my face. "Pee Wee did it. He hit me."

Mom carried me up the stairs to the kitchen. "Philip!" She yelled angrily. "Come here."

"I'm sorry Mom," he said, laughing apologetically. He grabbed a towel and wiped my hair. "It was a game. I didn't mean to hurt you Sis."

Mom grabbed Phil's hand, to get his attention. He looked at her.

"I tell you all the time to behave. Just wait…" Her voice trailed off. Until your father comes home, she was going to say, but that would be an empty threat because she had no idea if or when he would return. Instead she turned to me, "Why do you listen to him. Stay away."

"But he's my brother." I pleaded, my lip still quivering.

"You give me headache. I must lay down." It was Mom's only solution to conflict.

"It was funny," Ann whispered to Phil. "She deserved it, for tattling on us."

"Come on Sis. Ann and I will read you a story and I promise to buy you a sucker with the next penny I get," Bill said, taking my hand.

"Promise?"

"I promise."

During this time, Aunt Nadia's relative came to visit. "I have a cousin," she said to Mom. "He has a good job as a draftsman and works in Wheeling. A handsome Syrian man, and his name is Jim Casper. He wants to meet Marie."

"She is divorced and can't marry," Mom said.

"Lots of people divorce and remarry. This is not like the old country."

Marie and Jim met, and fell in love. He won Mom's heart, and she found it hard to object. "Maybe Allah will understand," she prayed. They were married by a justice of the piece.

"You stay with the Church," Mom cried. "Allah will bless you."

Marie took over the Pool Hall and made it into a short order restaurant and bar, named the Carlton. Entering, you were greeted with a beautiful cherry wood bar. The back wall had a large mirror, with a hand carved frame. There were booths on the opposite side. In the back was a dance floor with tables on each side. She employed her siblings, which improved the family income. Business was not great, with the economy so poor. The United States was in the worse depression of the century.

Dad began to drink excessively. If he ever came home sober, it didn't last. He lost interest in the family, the business, everything. His explosions of anger were incredible—he would blow up at everyone. As the days grew into months, his violent behavior became more extreme and frequent. It was intolerable and offensive. He would take the money Mom saved and go off for days. This was our way of life for the following year.

28

Nicolas, the dark side, 1934

Mom always held out hope—hope that Dad would return, somehow healed, and become the man he always dreamed he was. In reality that man had died a long time ago. But Mom did not accept this; at least she didn't seem to—not until the night that Dad came home drunk. I was five years old, and we had been playing at the dining room table.

"Five minutes more children and then you go to bed," Mom called from the kitchen. She was cleaning up and putting dishes away. "Every night I face the same problem," she thought. "Where to put the dishes? I miss the big house with the built in cupboard, a shelf for everything—plates, cups, bowls and serving dishes, all nicely displayed behind a beautiful mahogany, glass door. Now I have to leave my beautiful china on the sink. I hate this sink with its worn out painted wood drains, its chipped basin, and this blackened brass cold-water faucet. Not like my beautiful white enamel sink, with two copper faucets with ivory handles. I never knew what a luxury instant hot water was. The only thing new in this kitchen is the skirt I made for the sink front. I had to hide the pipes and my crock of *Arak*. Ime, this was not your dream for me. I never saw a cockroach before, now we have enough to start a circus. Like you, I never complain. Thank Allah we have our health."

Mom walked over to the dining room table and took a purple crayon out of my hand. "That's it, off to bed. Let me wipe the jelly off of your face."

"When will Daddy be back?" I asked.

"I don't know. Soon maybe." Then she thought, "How would I know? I haven't seen him for days."

"I want to tell him about the rat that bite me."

"That's all I need," Mama thought. "Tell Papa and he will blame me for letting you sleep with jelly on your face or for not standing guard. It's always my fault."

"It was funny, your lip squirted two streams of blood straight up like a V," Phil said. "It must have been a big rat. You cried enough."

"Not funny, it hurt. I hope the biggest rat in the world bites you," I shouted.

"That's enough. I can't take anymore. Get to bed," Mom ordered.

"Mama, can I sleep with you?"

"Yes."

"Good, she won't have to sleep with me," Ann cheered.

I stuck my tongue out at her.

"Put this on and climb into bed," Mom said handing me the nightgown. While I was changing, Mom got ready for bed. She took out her hairpins and laid them on the cedar chest, where she kept her mirror, comb, brush, and perfume. The room was too small for a dresser.

Lovingly she rubbed her hand over the beautiful piece of wood—a caress in her mind like fondling a baby. "It was my wedding gift from Nicolas," she thought. "I kept my wedding dress and all of my precious things from Syria. I have nothing left. My linens and my dress have all gone to make clothes for the children. Nicolas has sold all of my gold coins and jewelry. I'll never forget that day, that terrible day when those men came by. They were professional thieves and swindlers on the lookout for unsuspecting immigrants. They said we had to sell all our gold or we would get into trouble with the government. I said we don't have anything to sell. One man said, 'You foreigners all have gold.' Nicolas pushed me out of the away and took it all. Ann cried and grabbed the snake bracelet. How she cried. 'You promised this to me. You can't sell it.' I'm glad I told her to take it and hide. That's all that is left of my dowry, my Homeland."

"I have to stop thinking such things. Thank you Allah for our health, we will manage."

"Mama, tell me a story about Snef Snef," I asked.

"Okay, move over. First, we pray."

"In the name of the Father, the Son and the Holy Ghost," Mom said as she made the sign of the cross with the first three fingers, representing the Trinity. "My children are taught to use the whole hand with the thumb crossed over," Mom thought. "It doesn't make sense, but I don't argue. I won't change."

"God bless Mama, Daddy, everybody," I said looking up. "Please let me tell Daddy about the rat bite and don't let any more rats come when I sleep. Amen."

"Once there was a rich, arrogant, selfish dog named Snef Snef," Mom began. "He never helped anyone. One day he saw a hurt dog lying in the road."

"'Snef Snef, help me!' he begged."

"Snef Snef turned away and said, 'I can't be bothered.' Then he stopped at the well to get a drink. When he saw his reflection in the water, he smiled and climbed up on the rim to admire himself. He bent over and fell in."

"Did he drown, Mama?"

"No."

"He yelled, 'Help me! Help me!' But everyone that went by looked in the well and said, 'I can't be bothered'. Mom looked down at her sleeping daughter and then reached up to turn out the light. The chain was so short she had to stand on the bed. "I'll have to remember to tie a string on this," she thought. "Oh, the big house had lovely crystal switches."

Sleep came quickly for Mom. Within an hour or two, she was awakened by a disturbance. It was Daddy, carrying me to the couch in the living room. "It is a beautiful sight, Nicolas with his child," Mom thought. She laid her head back down on the pillow, comforted and happy.

Dad took off his jacket and slid into bed beside Mom. She could smell the familiar alcohol and smoke on his breath, the hallmark of a man. Mom looked at him lovingly and smiled.

He grabbed her hair, pulled her face into his and kissed her hard. His untrimmed mustache hung over his lip, his unshaven face was course and scratchy. She became frightened.

He pulled her head back by the hair, and his speech was slurred. "Why do you cheat on me? Who do you see? Karl?"

"No," Mom pleaded. "It isn't true. I would never sin against my family. Allah knows. How can you think such things?"

"Liar." He slapped her hard and she screamed with pain.

Then he pulled out a gun and held it against her head. Mom couldn't move. She closed her eyes and prayed.

"I'm going to kill you. I have the right, you adulteress."

"It's not true. There has never been anyone but you. We have nine children. How can you think such things? What have I done?" Her heart was pounding hard and fast. She could see me standing in the doorway, whimpering, covering my eyes and then running away.

"Daddy, Daddy's hurting Mama!" I cried, running to my brothers' bedroom.

The boys came running to our mother's defense. Mike and Paul grabbed Dad, and dragged him into the hallway, then threw him down to the floor. Jimmy took the gun. "Get out and don't come back," Paul said, tossing Dad's jacket in his face.

"I'll kill you, if you ever come near my mother again," Mike added.

"I'm your father, you can't do this," Dad said, struggling to get up.

"You're not my father!" Mike shouted. "Get out of here!"

Dad took his jacket and walked towards the stairs. Mike made a gesture to kick his father, but Paul held him back. Jimmy handed Mike the gun, "It's not loaded."

"He's crazy," Mike said. "That's the last we'll see of him."

The younger children came to see the commotion. Crying, I climbed up beside my mother and put my head on her shoulder. Mom couldn't move. Through all of this, she sat on her bed, petrified, unable to accept what was happening, unable to cry. Her children gathered around.

"Are you all right, Mom?" Jimmy asked.

She nodded. "Go back to bed. Everything will be all right. We'll talk about this in the morning."

"Ellen, come sleep with me," Teresa said, lifting me off of the bed. "Let Mama rest."

The older boys went into the kitchen, pulled out the crock from under the sink, ladled the Arak into a glass and passed it around. They poured some into another glass and Jimmy took it to Mom. She drank it down and climbed under the covers and cried hysterically. How could this happen? We are in America where everything is beautiful.

The house became quiet again as Mom lay there thinking. "What went wrong? Why? Ime," she cried. "My life isn't what we prayed for. Maybe, if we lived in Syria, money wouldn't have been so important. It broke Nicolas's spirit to loose all of that money. I don't understand what is happening. My husband tried to kill me, my son's turned on their father and my daughter is divorced. Did we sell our souls to live in America?"

"Ime, I need you now. I don't know what to do." She closed her eyes and tried to free her confused mind of all the guilt, but sleep would not come. Finally, her exhausted body relaxed. "Ime," she murmured in her sleep.

Her body felt weightless, floating through space. When she opened her eyes she was in her mother's kitchen. "Ime, you're here, wearing the bracelet and making bread. I'm always so small when I'm with you."

Ime put down the dough and went to the hot clay oven. There were two small copper Turkish coffee pots, with long handles. One held hot milk and the other contained black, strong coffee, sweetened with honey. She brought them to the table and simultaneously poured them into a small bowl like cup, then handed it to her daughter. Mom drank the coffee as fast as she could, then inverted the cup into the saucer and anxiously awaited her mother's next move.

Ime picked up the cup. "You are a strong woman. I see a family wheel. The children are the spokes and the father is the hub. The mother is the rim, holding it all together. But the hub is broken. You must see that the spokes reach across the hub to hold hands, stay in place, and drive the wheel."

As fast as Ime had appeared, she was gone.

"What does it mean?" Mom could hear herself saying as she woke up. "Ime, come back."

Restlessly, she lay in bed trying to remember her strange dream and what it meant. "I will ask Marie. She is smart. She'll know."

The children woke up to the aroma of fresh coffee brewing and sweet, comforting bread baking. Mom had taken the raw dough, which she always kept in the ice box, for just such an occasion. She patted it flat, brushed it with butter, sprinkled cinnamon and sugar, rolled it up and sliced it into pin wheels.

Phil, the first to arrive in the kitchen, exclaimed, "Cinnamon rolls!"

"You must respect him," Mom said, pouring coffee for the boys. "He's your father."

"Not mine," Mike protested.

"He will always be your father. I want you to give him a room on the second floor. He won't be any bother, and he will have a place to live."

"You'll probably send him food," Mike added.

"Of course," Mom said, pouring more coffee.

"He better not come up here."

After breakfast, Mom went to visit Marie. "I saw Ime in my dream."

"Again?"

"Yes, she said the family is a wheel, the children are the spokes, Papa the hub and me the rim."

"That figures."

"What?"

"You the rim, holding everything together and the one we roll over," Marie said. "You suffer the most."

"I don't understand."

"Some dreams aren't meant to be understood," Marie said. They're just dreams. You are a strong woman and you will have to be the Papa now. My health is not good. The doctor said I need a dry, warm climate. I have chronic bronchitis and this weather is bad for me. Mama, we are going to move to the desert."

"You have to?"

"Yes, if I want to live."

"I'll miss you and Joey."

"We will be back for a visit, and you can come see us."

When I heard the news that Marie and Joey would be moving I cried. Joey and I were very close, we were best friends. He was very enterprising at an early age, and at seven, he persuaded me to learn a song, *The Isle of Capri.*

"Would you like to hear us sing for you?" he asked Mr. Shaheen, who owned an ice-cream parlor. We sang with the enthusiasm of Metropolitan Opera stars. The customers clapped and Mr. Shaheen gave us each an ice-cream cone.

"Next time," Joey said, "we will add a dance, for two scoops of ice-cream."

"Okay, you're hired. You should be a lawyer some day," Mr. Shaheen said smiling.

Joey choreographed the dance as we acted out the words of the song. I had to sit on a bench as Joey walked by singing *It was on the Isle of Capri where I met her.* I invitingly dropped my handkerchief. Joey retrieved it, knelt down, kissed my hand and saw a cigar wrapper ring on my finger. He tearfully walked away, singing, *It's good bye to the Isle of Capri.* The first performance brought us three scoops of ice-cream.

"Joey, I'm going to miss you," I said. "I'll never sing again."

"I know, I don't want to go, but my Mom is sick. You can come to visit us, and maybe I'll come back here."

Within months, they packed up and headed south. When they arrived in Birmingham, Alabama, short of their destination, they decided to stay long enough to replenish their funds. Jim got a good job and they never left.

Dad moved in downstairs and Mom often sent special dishes of food he liked. He also ate at the Carlton. He acted like nothing was wrong. When people praised him for his wonderful children, he accepted the credit.

Mom had an inner strength that she was unaware of. She handled the family finances and made all of the decisions for providing food and clothing. She paid off Dad's debts.

"Mom," Teresa said. "We can put slot-machines in the Carlton. It will make a lot of money."

"That would be gambling. I don't know if it is right. Is it a sin?"

Teresa walked over to her mother. "It's legal."

"I will pray," Mom said. "If it is a sin, let it be mine."

29

The father I knew, 1942

My father as I knew him was different from the dashing young suitor my mother married. He was born and reared in Lebanon, the younger of two children, David was the older. His father was very strict and not particularly loving. His mother was affectionate and proud of her boys, but she was frail and became an invalid the last few years of her life.

My father attended school until the age of thirteen and then joined his brother working in a clothing store. He was frustrated working for a family where the older men made all the decisions, leaving little opportunity for a bright young man to make a significant contribution. It must have seemed like a hopeless situation. That and the political unrest with the Ottoman Turks in power may have been the reasons my father came to America. He had high aspirations, driven to succeed in business, a workaholic. I think that he was hurt by discrimination. He always said, "You must work harder than anyone else, because they think that Arabs are lazy. We show them."

My father made his mark in America. He became rich, investing in property, stocks and bonds. My siblings enjoyed talking about the "good old days," and how Dad was a loving husband, and a generous father. He flaunted his wealth, and would tell his brothers-in-law, "You will never get rich owning a restaurant. Get smart, buy stocks, and buy property. You think like the old country." Wealth made Dad a proud, if not an arrogant man.

Unfortunately my father lacked the ability to analyze the economic trends. He did not foresee the dangers of Wall Street, and ignored the violent upswings in the market. He was devastated by the economic crash, and never recovered. Like most people suffering from depression, I doubt if Dad knew why he was depressed. I think that he was troubled by guilt—why he didn't take more precautions. He often said, "I should have covered my bets." Dad was rich and poor before I was born. Knowing these early circumstances helped me to understand him.

I missed knowing the affectionate, fun loving father—the one who playfully hugged my mother, and teased the girls. I never saw Dad kiss Mom, but then the Syrian men I knew were never demonstrative.

The father I knew was basically shy and not good at personal relationships. He no longer associated with Karl, and often secluded himself from the world. The first few years of my life, I remember Dad being well dressed, often with a suit and tie. I thought he was handsome. When he lived alone, his clothes were messy and sometimes dirty. As bad as it was then, his depression was not as extreme as it became later.

I suspect that he was always controlling, making decisions on his own, and telling Mom after the fact. During this period, he became very dominating with a fierce temper. No one questioned him. I often wished that he would be reasonable. If I asked for a nickel to buy some candy, and he said no, I wondered if he was angry or broke, but I never asked.

He was an absentee father, and was not there when I was born, my graduation, nor any time I needed him, but I loved him. Dad was more gentle and kind with the girls. He would back hand his sons for raising their voice but never touched his daughters. As a child, I would climb on his lap and listen to the radio. He was tranquilized. It was like sitting on a statue. He never spoke or smiled. There were rare moments when he was happy. The family would talk about the past, when Dad would have watermelon-seed spiting contests and relays at the park.

I remember Mom trying desperately to reassure Dad that everything would be all right. She would rub his back in hopes of alleviating the stress, but to no avail. I had no idea what was happening and didn't recognize the signs of depression—overwhelming doubt about himself, his abilities, and his wife. They never labeled his disorder. Later in college I became familiar with the illness called manic-depression. It fit his symptoms. His mood swings went from violent destruction, to almost a catatonic state.

Early on, I think that Dad was family oriented, despite his combative relationship with his brothers-in-law. I often heard them disagree on everything. My Uncles spoke of my father with some condescension. "You a big shot spend money like water," Uncle Tom would say.

They never spoke kindly of each other. When Dad lost everything, Hashar said, "What did you expect, you never saved any money. For a smart man you are dumb."

I frequently visited Dad in his apartment downstairs and took food that Mom made. I loved telling on Phil, (Pee Wee) and Ann to get them in trouble, and they always picked on me. I told Dad about the Epsom salt prank.

"The other day, when Mom had errands to run she left me with Pee Wee and Ann," I said. "Mom told them not to let me get into the sugar. She put the bowl up on the cupboard shelf. I love to get into the sugar bowl and eat it by the handfuls."

"It's not good for you," Dad said. "Why do you do that?"

"Cause it tastes so sweet. I heard Ann say, 'Maybe we can cure her.' While Pee Wee kept me busy in the dining room, Ann slipped into the kitchen, dumped the sugar from the bowl into a cup, filled the bowl with Epsom salt and put it back on the shelf. Then she spread a piece of bread with butter and sugar, and shared it with us. I wanted some more, but Ann said, 'Get it yourself.' So I went into the kitchen and climbed up the cupboard. Dad, did you ever see me climb?"

Dad smiled. "You could get hurt. Mama doesn't like you to do that."

"I held on to one shelf, and lifted my foot up, and climbed, one at a time. When I reached the sugar, I dipped into the bowl, and grabbed as much as my little hand could hold. I tried to protect it in my fist, but it was hard to climb backwards with one hand. So I stopped on the second shelf, and looked at my treasure. It sparkled in my hand. I shoved the whole thing into my mouth, and cried, Yuck! It wasn't sugar, and it tasted awful. I was crying and spitting, and fell backwards. Pee Wee caught me, and said, 'What's the matter?' like he didn't know. I was crying and spitting at the same time, and I told him that I ate poison. Ann grabbed my hand, and smelled the stuff. She said, 'It's poison alright.'"

"You thought it was poison?" Dad asked.

"Ann said I was going to die, and she wanted me to will her my music box. I didn't want to die. I cried harder, burying my head in the floor, spitting and choking. I begged Pee Wee to help me. He was nice and gave me a glass of water. He said, it wasn't poison, and I would be alright. What is Epsom salt?" I asked.

"That's what your mother uses to soak my feet," Dad said.

"Then Ann emptied the sugar bowl, rinsed it out and put the sugar back," I continued. "When Mom came home, Pee Wee told her that I got into the Epson salt because I thought it was sugar. Mom yelled at me. She said that God punished me for trying to sneak sugar. It's not fair, they didn't get into trouble."

"Don't play with them," Dad said. "I think they are jealous of you."

"But I don't have anyone to play with." Dad comforted me, and the next time he saw Ann and Pee Wee he scolded them.

When I graduated from eighth grade, my father gave me a beautiful gold-filled bracelet. "You like it?" he asked. "I give it to you, if you promise never to get married."

"Daddy, I can promise not to marry before I'm twenty-one maybe, but never? I don't think so," I said, returning the gift. "Why do you ask?"

"Keep the bracelet. You think about it." He never explained his feelings.

When we moved to another house, my father continued to live at the hotel, I saw less and less of him. During my high-school years, my relationship with Dad continued to diminish, as he lost interest in me and the family. He drank more, and kept to himself in his room. I saw him occasionally downtown or at the Carlton. We never really visited. I had no one to lean on. I think that my ambivalent attitude toward men came from my estranged relationship with my father.

When I got married, my father gave me away. At the reception, Mom said, "Ask your father to dance. He is a good dancer and use to be the life of the party."

I walked over to Dad and wrapped my veil around his neck. "Dance with me. We do the *dubkee.*" Without a word, he shook his head no. I sat on his lap with my arms around him, and he smiled. My sister grabbed me and we danced. I think that was the last warm feeling I had toward my father. I moved to California, and never wrote or sent pictures of my children.

30

Maheeba's stroke and recovery,
1941

In May, 1941, about ten o'clock in the morning, after everyone had gone to work or school, mom's health finally gave out. She had been making up the bed when suddenly she felt faint. Trying to regain her balance, mom grabbed the blanket, but her legs gave way and she slid to the floor, pulling the bed cover with her. Unable to cry out she could only lay there listening to the sounds of people talking and walking from the floor below.

Paul came home about an hour later, sounding his arrival, "Mom I'm home. Where are you?" Finding her in the bedroom, he yelled, "Mom!" She was lying on the floor, her eyes were open, but she couldn't speak. He called the fire department and they took her to the hospital. The children were summand home from school. Teresa went to St. Anthony's to get me. Mother Superior called me to the office. "Your sister is here to take you home," she said. "Your mother is ill."

I was twelve years old, and so confused. "Mom was never sick," I thought. "Teresa's taking me out of school. It must be serious. Was she dead?" I was too frightened to ask. "Please God, don't let her die."

"What happened?" I asked.

"Mom's in the hospital. We don't know how serious. I'll take you there."

"Let's say a prayer," Sister said, kneeling down with us. I began to cry.

"I sent for my brother Jimmy at the CCC Camp, and he's coming home on an emergency leave," Teresa said to Sister.

"We will pray for you at Chapel tonight," Sister said.

The diagnosis was a massive stroke brought on by stress and high blood pressure. Mom lay in the hospital for weeks, no movement, and no voice. She could open her eyes but was otherwise lifeless.

"The damage is extensive," the doctor said, consulting with the family. "Her right side is paralyzed, her speech is impaired and there is some memory loss. We will have to keep her in the hospital until she responds. When she does, there is physical therapy that might help to regain some use of her arm and leg. It is going to be a long haul."

We all gathered in her room, crying and talking at the same time.

"Who are these people?" Mom thought.

Our voices like a roaring wave, pounded against her ears and then slipped quietly back into the ocean. "You will have to leave," the nurse said. "We can allow only two to three people at the most."

"Does she hear us?" Teresa asked.

"Yes, but she may not remember you. You will have to talk to her, which will be a big help." So we did, and Mom was never without family.

Hashar would visit every day, sit for hours and talk to her. "Maheeba, my little sister, come back, we miss you," he said holding her hand in his. "Do you remember when you were little, Papa would stand you on the table, you would move your hands back and forth, like you were cleaning the house and sing *Heck, heck*...like this, like this your house is clean and neat. You would sway back and forth and turn around. You were beautiful, like Ime. You would sing and dance for us all the time."

Her eyes would lock on his face and when he moved, they dragged along. "Who is this person?" Mom asked herself. "Do I know him?"

"When we were cutting wheat in the field," Hashar said, "you would sneak up, hide and make a noise. What is that?" Papa would say. "Maybe it's a big mouse?"

Mom's mind merged with his voice and became one. "I can see the fields. I'm a little girl hiding," she thought. "I make squeaking sounds. Papa and Hashar have a big knife. I peek to see if they are looking."

"I would tell Papa that maybe it's a big snake," Hashar continued. "We better run, and then you come out laughing. You were a good girl. When I was milking the goat, you would lay down so I could squirt milk in your mouth. I think the goat thought you were her baby. Remember how *Bashada* would hold you on his shoulders so you could pick the apricots on top? They were the biggest and the sweetest. You never made me mad, even when you ran away with Nicolas. I wasn't mad at you. I prayed to Allah, keep you safe and bring you back."

A Mona Lisa smile came over her face. "I see the house and the date trees," she thought. "I miss fresh dates. We don't have fresh dates any more but I remember the taste."

When the nurse walked in, Hashar moved, "Don't get up, I just have a few things to do. It is good to talk to her."

"I don't know, she never moves, only her eyes."

As the children visited, one by one, they would say their name. "Mom, I'm Paul, your son. Uncle Frank is coming to visit tomorrow. He asks about you every day."

"I know you," she thought. "I see you before."

When it was my turn to visit, I sat there holding her hand. "What should I say? I didn't bring anything to read. Mom, I've always wanted to tell you this. I thought about it a lot. Do you remember my first day at school? I was going into first grade, and you bought me a new outfit. It was a red polka dot dress with a white collar and white satin belt. I wore long tan stockings with black patent leather shoes. I remember everything. Pee Wee offered to walk me to school, and on the way, he told me that Sister Angela would have everybody go up in front of the room and say their name."

'You can be the only one to spell your name because it is so easy,' he said. "Ellen is <u>P I G</u>. Sister will be so surprised that she will probably send a note home to Mom.'

"I believed him. He coaxed me to repeat the spelling, Ellen P I G Ellen, and I learned how to spell pig. He was really nice to me. When we arrived at the playground, I remember grabbing his hand. All those big kids running around, it was scary. Almost everyone had their mother, but I had my big brother and that was okay. Pee Wee walked me to the classroom, and then left. Sister Angela took my hand and led me to a seat. She put all the first graders on the right side of the room, and the second graders on the left." As I talked, I began to recall so many details. "Sister wrote her name on the black board. The parents had to leave, and one little girl began to cry. Sister said that we would take turns going to the front of the room, and saying our names. Just like Pee Wee said. One by one the children gave their full name. I thought my brother must be the smartest boy in the whole world. When it was my turn, I stood up, straightened my dress and took my place in the front of the class. My name is Ellen Thomas and I can spell it, Ellen P I G Ellen. The second graders began to laugh."

'Honey, that's not how you spell your name,' Sister said.

"Yes it is my brother told me."

'He was teasing you,' she said. 'That spells pig. It was a mean prank.'

"No it isn't," I said. "You're a liar, and I don't like you. She was so mad. Then Sister shook me, and asked for my brother's name. I told her, Phil Thomas and he'll show you. Sister sent for Pee Wee, and she yelled at him. She said that he should be ashamed of himself, and told him that I called her a liar. Sister sent us both home. Pee Wee told me not to tell you. He said that I could go to Hell for talking to a Nun like that. When we got home, and you asked what happened, Pee Wee said that I was sent home for misspelling my name. Mom, I don't know if you want to hear this—I called a Nun a liar, but when I made my First Communion, I went to confession and told the priest everything. I did my penance. It's okay now."

Mom looked at me, and frowned as though she was trying to make sense out of what I was saying. I'm not sure she understood, because she never mentioned it.

Uncle Frank came the next day. "I'm going to open my own restaurant," he said. Rose has been saving for ten years. She cleans out my pockets when I come home drunk. Then she hides the money. We have enough to buy the equipment but we'll rent for awhile. We named it the Temple. It is in the Masonic building. We'll serve breakfast and lunch to business people. It has an ice-cream parlor for afternoon business. No dinner. I will be the cook. You taught me good. We miss you. Do you remember when we went to the movie on Ellis Island? I thought the cowboys were going to shoot us and I knocked you to the floor?"

A smile came over her face, and then she tried to speak.

"She's smiling." Frank called to the others in the room.

"What?" he asked, putting his ear to her lips.

"Keef…?" she muttered.

"How am I? Good. Allah be praised."

Mom closed her eyes. This was the beginning of her limited recovery. For the next few weeks, she retired into herself, like she was waiting to wake up from a terrible dream. "A big miracle will happen," she thought, "and it will be yesterday again."

Dad asked about Mom all the time. When I visited him, he spoke about the old times. "Your mother was beautiful," he said. "She could dance and sing like an angel. Will she come home soon?"

"I don't know," I said. "She remembers us, but she can't talk very well."

"I want to see her," Dad said. "I have to talk to her."

"I'll ask the boys. Maybe Jimmy will take you."

"I think Dad should see Mom," Jimmy said. "I'll take him."

When they arrived at the hospital, Jimmy said, "I'll be in the waiting room. Just take your time." He believed that Dad still loved Mom, and that she loved him too.

Dad brought her lilacs. "Here," he said. "Is this still your favorite flower?"

Mom took it with her left hand, and held the bouquet to her face, remembering happier times.

"How do you feel?" Dad asked.

She nodded. "Did you eat?"

"Yes, I ate at the Carlton. Not so good. Not like you cook. I miss your meat pies and kibby. You will cook again."

Mom smiled. "I wish I could talk," she thought. "There's so much I want to say. I want to tell you that things are better now. The boys went to CCC camp, and sent half of their check home every month. You would be proud."

Dad held her hand. "Why did this happen?" he said with tears in his eyes. "Do you remember what they sang at our wedding? *Because God made Thee mine,* you said it was the most beautiful song you ever heard. I bought you the music, and you cried because you couldn't read."

"Yes." Mom closed her eyes and smiled, reliving the time and the music. "Why can't we go back to happier times?" It was the last time they were together, until the end of World War 11.

31

World War 11, December 7, 1941

Mom responded very well to therapy and was able to walk with a cane. Her left arm hung like a broken branch on a tree. Concentrating all her strength and straining, she could raise her arm about eight inches and then it would drop. After three months, she announced, "No more, I do no more exercises. If God wants me to use my arm He will make a miracle." But He never did.

December 7, 1941, the day that would "live in infamy" changed the lives of the Thomas family.

"Extra, extra read all about it," the newspaper boys shouted in the street below. Teresa shut the window so Mom wouldn't hear. Everyone nervously tried to avoid discussing the situation in front of Mom. We whispered behind closed doors "We will be in and out of war in no time," Jimmy said, "a couple of months."

"It will take us that long to get ready," Phil said.

"I'm going to enlist," Mike said, "so I can join the air force."

"What about Mom," Ann said. "I think the news could give her a heart attack."

We decided it was best not to tell Mom that President Roosevelt had declared war. This seemed like an almost impossible secret to keep. The boys were drafted one by one, Tom Tom was exempt. Mom was told that they were going to CCC camp. For almost a year, Mom did not know that World War 11 had erupted.

Jimmy joined the Merchant Marines, and each furlough he gave mom the bonus he received. Paul and Mike went into the air force, and Phil the army. The boys agreed to save a percentage of their monthly check to pay off the seven thousand dollar mortgage on the hotel.

With the boys gone, Teresa ran the Carlton. During that time, a neighbor lady, Mazeeda visited every day. She was a composite of distasteful characteristics.

Her breasts rested on her fat stomach. She was crude, wearing profanity as a badge of honor and dedicated to embarrassing everyone. She would pat the little girls on the breast, and say, "You flat, like boy." Then she would grab the crotch, and say, "No, you girl." She was a stranger to body soap, even though Teresa showered her with perfume, scented soap, powder and deodorant.

"Have you tried the shampoo?" Teresa asked.

"One, maybe two Saturdays."

"In a month? I'll give you some more, if you promise to wash your hair every week."

"No! Make gray."

Her black greasy hair smelt sour from the humidity. "Mazeeda, you can't wash out the color in your hair."

"No like gray. Madoon, I come to see you, we play cards."

"Why do you call my Mom Madoon?" I asked.

"A pet name, she's my pet."

"Mom and Uncle Hashar are in the kitchen."

"Good, we play *basala*. Tom Tom come play cards, no cheat."

The four of them played cards for hours. Then Mazeeda got up, threw the cards across the table. "I loose one game, two, three, you cheat. I no come back."

"Please stay. Nobody cheat. We'll let you win," Mom pleaded.

"No. I go."

"You won two games," Tom Tom said. "You're the one who cheats, signaling with your fingers."

"I never come back," Mazeeda said, shaking her head and walking out the door.

The next day, Mazeeda returned. "Maheeba, my Madoon. My heart breaks. Where are you?"

"What? Why you cry?"

"My boy Joseph, he goes to war."

"What you say?" Mom struggled with her words.

"The war. My baby drafted, see." She flashed a piece of paper.

"War? What war?"

"We fight Japan. Our children all gone."

"No," Mom said. "My boys at camp."

"No camp, army."

"You crazy! Ann you come," Mom called.

Ann came into the room to find both women crying. "What is going on?"

"Tell true. We in war," Mazeeda said.

"You big mouth. Why did you have to tell?"

"My boy goes in the army," Mazeeda said. "Like your brothers."

"Mom, I'm sorry. The war has been going on for almost a year. The boys are fine. We didn't want you to worry. Now you know. Wait a minute. I have something to give you." Ann left the room and returned with a blue velvet scroll pennant. "This is to hang in our window. There are four gold stars, one for each boy."

"I get one for my boy?" Mazeeda asked.

During the war, business flourished. The Carlton installed slot machines which tripled the family income. Teresa found a beautiful house with a big yard for sale, two miles from town. "Mom, there's this house for sale. It's the Cowan place. I think we can buy it. I talked to Uncle Tom. He thinks it's a good buy."

Teresa dreamed about the beautiful red brick house for a week. It had a big back yard with apple trees. The front porch was the length of the house, perfect for Mom and Uncle Hashar to visit. It had two stories with five bedrooms, three fireplaces, a basement and attic. Financing in place, Teresa finally went to the owner. She noticed that the *For Sale* sign was gone. She knocked, and a man answered. "I have the money, we want to buy."

He shook his head. "I sold it, to Tom Bakeer. He said you didn't want it."

"I did, I do want it."

"I thought it was strange." Mr. Cowan said. "He offered me more money. I'm sorry."

Teresa went away, sad and angry. The next day, she confronted Uncle Tom. "How could you buy the house behind my back? How could you do that? You knew how much I wanted that house. Mom wanted it. You cheat your own sister?"

"It's too big for your family. There's a nice one on Main Street. You look at it, maybe buy."

"If I were a man, or my brothers were here, you would never do this."

Disappointed but determined, Teresa found a beautiful house on the outskirts of town. It had a lovely front door with beveled glass. There were five bedrooms upstairs and a sun room with a bed on the first floor for Mom. The big, bright, living and dining rooms each had a fireplace. It had a barn, converted into a garage and a lot which extended to the river. In many ways it was better suited to the family. She bought it.

"Cora, help me pick out some furniture. I want all new things, except Mom's cedar chest and china closet."

"What about all the stuff at the hotel?"

"I'm going to rent the rooms out. Dad wants to live on the third floor."

"I'll get you a beautiful set of dishes from work. I get a discount."

They added a bath to Mom's bedroom on the first floor. It looked like a shrine, with all the statues and candles. She kissed each Saint every night and never slighted anyone. Mom lived happily in the confines of her home, protected by her children.

Before the war ended, the man who owned the bookies on the second floor of the hotel gave notice that he was leaving. "I want to retire," he said. "When my lease runs out, I'll quit."

"What will you do with the equipment?"

"Sell it."

"How much?"

"Seven hundred dollars. Why? Women aren't allowed in this joint."

"I want to buy it for my brothers. I'll give you a hundred dollars a month."

"Okay. I'll draw up the papers."

The boys came home to a new life and a new home. Jimmy helped the girls manage the Carlton. The other four boys ran the Bookies.

Mom insisted that all her boys come home for dinner. She said to her daughter, "You be good girls. Go work. Send your brothers home."

Ann or Teresa relieved Jimmy. The Bookies closed at five o'clock.

"Mom, we are taking you to the Carlton for a special party," Jimmy said. "Ann will get you dressed."

"What surprise?"

"You'll see."

When they arrived, there was a big table set up in the middle of the dance floor. It was dressed with flowers and a white linen cloth. As Mom was being seated, Dad walked in.

"Sit, sit." She invited.

He smiled and sat across from her.

"Mom, this piece of paper is the mortgage on the building," Paul said. He took out his lighter and set fire to the last bad memory. "This framed document is the title. We now own it free and clear."

32

Maheeba's funeral, 1958

Late summer was the most beautiful time of the year in the Ohio Valley. The trees were transformed into multi-colored rainbows; apples were ripe and ready for picking. Gigantic sunflowers drooped over from the weight of their seeds. Bundles of hay were scattered throughout the fields, and the air was warm and crisp.

I'm sure my mother, with her heavenly connections above, ordered this setting, and orchestrated the entire event. It was her funeral.

My mother's death, which brought us here, began with a vigil for two days. My siblings never left the mortuary. The flowers overflowed into the waiting room and hall. "These are the most flowers I have ever seen," said the attendant. "Everybody loved your mother." I think he was trying to comfort us. My brothers purchased the most expensive coffin available. It was well padded for comfort with a cream colored satin lining. She looked beautiful in her new navy-blue dress with a yellow flower design. My mother held her crystal rosaries in her hand and wore the relic of the "true cross" around her neck. I knelt down and kissed it, remembering her wearing it underneath her clothes and putting it under her pillow at night.

Once when she was changing the linen wrapping, I saw the relic. It was a piece of wood about three inches long and two inches wide, not much bigger than a sliver. To Mom it symbolized Christ's suffering. I believe she gained comfort and strength from it.

I could not embrace Mom's faith in the relic. It defies all logic. Jesus wasn't the last person to be crucified on that cross, and I doubt if the Christians at that time would have considered the cross a memento. Today, in Israel, you can buy a similar relic blessed by a Priest. I could not believe that Mom's sliver of wood was from the "true cross," and survived the ages. No one in the family wanted the responsibility of being care taker of the relic, and it was buried with my mother.

A parade of cars carrying family and friends followed the black Carriage. My sister Marie held my hand, and said, "When you were born, we went to the hospital in a hearse, but it wasn't so fancy. Not many people begin their life in a hearse."

We gathered at the top of a knoll, and looked down over the beautiful green valley. It was the most scenic spot in the cemetery. My brothers had purchased about ten plots, so the family could be remembered together in death as in life. I could feel my mother's presence, and see her smile. Every time we had visited the site, she would pat the plot of ground next to my father, as though she were testing a bed for firmness, and brush off any debris. "This is for me," she would claim, smiling.

Mom visited the grave sites of her loved ones every holiday. Suddenly, I felt that this was very morbid. "I don't want my children to be responsible for maintaining a place that houses my decayed body," I thought. My generation was becoming more mobile, leaving the place of their birth to seek job opportunities. Each of my children had been born in a different state on the west coast.

My mother was placed next to my father. A few feet away were Tom Tom, who had died at age fifty: a twenty-one year old nephew killed in an accident, and an infant nephew I had never seen. It was a short stroll down the hillside to where Aunt Confidad and Uncle Hashar were buried. My uncle spent his last days, sitting on the porch swing with my mother. I could sit beside them, reading, for hours, and never hear them utter a word. Yet I felt the strength of their love, and the comfort of each others presence. If one spoke, it was in short phrases. "Remember when....?" or, "Market day....?" The other one would nod, as though the memories they shared, were categorized by cue words.

Confidad, whom we called Umtee, will always be remembered as the healer. Her remedy for a headache was a cold coin, quarter or half-dollar, placed firmly on the forehead. I remember, the room would be dark, and she would hum softly while rubbing my head. "You never take aspirin, God will heal," Mom would say. If He didn't, you offered it up to the poor souls in Purgatory.

My sisters and I clung together tightly, bracing ourselves against the chill of death. Looking at my brothers, I saw grown men crying, for the first time in my life. My grief was tempered with the thought that my mother was no longer in pain. For two years she had suffered with cancer. We watched the lump on her neck grow, because she refused to go to the hospital. In the final stage, the doctor came to the house, and treated her for pain. I had seen my mother two months earlier, when I, my husband and two daughters, came to visit. Her bedroom was like a shrine, filled with statues. Every night she kissed each one, not to slight any saint. It was heart breaking to see this frail person, with bones merely covered by flesh, her pale cheeks hollow. She was unrecognizable. My daughter looked at her and said, "Is this my grandma?" Mom motioned for me to lift up her pillow and pull out a handkerchief, which held six dollars. I opened it up and Mom took the money. Her voice was barely audible, "Call me Tata," she said, as she smiled and handed the money to the girls. Then she swiped one hand over the other, gesturing a clean sweep. "Is that the last of your money?" I asked, and she nodded, "yes." I felt that Mom held on for this moment, and now she was ready to depart.

"Always work hard, and do a little more," was my mother's daily pep talk. I worked hard and did a lot more than expected. Why couldn't I take pride in my accomplishments? Was it because, my mother made me feel that pride in a woman was a sin?

"Be a good Syrian woman," Mom would say, "or God will punish you." Her Allah was a vengeful God, who could be bargained with. I still wanted to be an American. Here, at her grave site, I looked over all of Maheeba's living descendents; her grandchildren and great grandchildren. These were America's affluent children, born in the mid-twentieth century, and destined to flourish in the twenty-first.

People react in different ways to death, especially the death of a parent. My mother's death left me confused, because most of what I felt between us was about myself, and how she affected me. Now that was gone, and I became a part of the older generation. I believe that my close, loving relationship with my mother made my grief deeper and simpler. Yet I remain troubled, why did she leave me with such ambivalent feelings of who I am? I doubt my self worth, by dwelling on my failures. In 1980, when I received my doctorate, I could only guess that my mother would have said, "What a waste of time."

A plain granite tombstone marked her passing.

Maheeba, Mabel Thomas
Born: July 10, 1894
Died: July 28, 1958

She was survived by eight of nine children, each dressed in black. My mother had listed the steps that must be taken by children to assure eternal peace for their loved ones. To honor the dead, there must be a wake for at least two days, to provide the time for intense grieving. Wailing, screaming, pulling at your clothes, throwing your body on the grave were all acceptable displays of torment. My mother left her children this blueprint of a custom not practiced in America.

We followed every detail for her funeral. There were enough relatives to replace the professional mourners. Among them were a couple of old Syrian women crying out, "Allah is with you."

One of them threw herself on the coffin screaming. She was in her late fifties and not unattractive. My brothers tried to comfort and help her walk toward me. She was so limp, they had to carry her. "She must be in agony," I thought as I got up to give her my seat. I was so moved that I wanted to embrace her. Before I could speak, she sat up, took out her compact and fixed her make-up. She put on lipstick, smiled and wiped the corners of her mouth. All I could say was, "A remarkable recovery." No one else seemed to notice.

I was mortified but knew it was a Syrian custom. They were just acting according to expectations. This whole drama had been scripted by Mom.

The graveside ceremony was brief, and among the biggest funerals ever held there. Everyone returned to the house for the reception. It was a celebration of life. Heavy drinking and toasting the memory of the deceased was an absolute requirement. For twelve hours they ate, drank and remembered.

For me it was endless torment. I put my grief on hold, to maintain a façade of composure. I could not find a place to hide or even a moment alone. Someone always found me.

"You must be present," my Aunt said. It's expected of the family."

"Haven't we suffered enough?" I asked. "I just want to be left alone." It was barbaric and I vowed not to leave such a legacy to my children. "I shall be a body donor," I vowed, and Stanford University will dispose of the remains—as different from this ceremony as possible.

So we bury the dead body, and embrace their spirit. My children never knew my mother as I never knew my grandmother, but I can write about these women, because of all the stories they shared. If I am a caretaker, it is because of my mother. If I share my joy, and hide my grief, it is because of my mother. If I cater to men and judge women too harshly, it is because of my mother. If I am ambitious, and materialistic, it is because of my mother. These are the characteristics I pass on to my children—American values and tradition, spiced with the mid Eastern culture.

From the Middle East to Middle America, my mother's life bridged two cultures, as has my life in some ways.

0-595-31525-9

Printed in the United States
18560LVS00006B/112-138